BREAKING FREE

**How to Be Completely Free
from Any Addiction**

by Kevin W. Shorter

ACKNOWLEDGEMENTS

This book would not have been possible without the loving support of my wife, Allison. She entered into her fear and pain instead of running away from my addiction. Her loving commitment to me gave me strength to continue on when I felt I had nothing else. I could not have imagined how wonderful marriage could be when we first met 20 years ago. I also can't imagine loving you anymore than I do, but each year I find that I love you more than before. I love you!

There have been a number of men in my life that have helped me in this process. I would never be able to mention them all, but there a few I need to single out. To Neal Huggins and Andy Creekmore, you have known me since elementary school and liked me even then. Neal, you showed me how to communicate. Our clandestine night walks were foundational in how I still approach relationships. Andy, you taught me how to live with someone else. I saw you value our friendship over many frustrations I caused you. I had never considered how to value others over myself before.

To Steve Hopper, thank you for continuing to pursue our friendship over many moves and many life transitions. God has used you to draw out so much in me. Thank you for always making time.

To Jeff Veal, I have never connected with someone so quickly and completely as you. You know my deepest darkest and yet you still make me feel that I can conquer the world. Thank you.

CONTENTS

1

HOW IS THIS BOOK DIFFERENT?

Long Time Coming

This book has taken a long time to come about. For someone who has struggled with addiction, writing a book about how to be completely clean is daunting. Even though I had gone through a God-experience that completely changed my life, I had struggled for many years and feared appearing a hypocrite to write a book like this.

However, the truth is, this book was the final step in my process of healing. My God-experience virtually freed me, but there were still lingering temptations I had not conquered before completing this book. It was like God was asking me to start the book by faith and trust Him to meet me on the way.

There was also the fear of becoming the "addiction guy". If I wrote a book on addiction, I would be forever linked to my struggles with my personal addiction, pornography. My embarrassment had kept me from telling close friends; did I now want to openly proclaim my struggles?

Still, somehow the book and my complete healing were inextricably tied. I put off writing the book for many years because I had experienced such healing that minor stumbles were endurable. However, as time went on, I grew increasingly uncomfortable when I faltered. It became more and more apparent that this book was in my future.

I won't get into all the reasons why I believe this book was necessary for my freedom, but I will share one of the stories that God used to motivate me: David and Goliath.

David and Goliath

Many people in this struggle with addiction identify with the story of David and Goliath. They see the hold addiction has on them and relate to the Israelites who were paralyzed with fear. Goliath was a terror to Israel, standing between the nation and its God-declared destiny. Like Israel, those struggling with addiction feel they are powerless to overcome their struggles and enter the freedom Jesus promises.

In my own struggle, God had empowered me to attack this Philistine and finish him off. I had slung the stone and saw Goliath fall, but I had yet to do as David had – take my enemy's sword and cut off his head.

David grabbed the sword meant to keep all of Israel in fear and destroyed his enemy. The source of Israel's disgrace became the tool for ultimate victory. This is what God has for you in your struggle with addiction. You will overcome the enemy by the blood of Jesus and *the word of your testimony* (Rev. 12:11).

David refused to use King Saul's sword because it was too cumbersome for him wield. But when it came to Goliath's sword, David quickly removed Goliath's head. When we defeat our personal demons, we are given new tools to advance God's kingdom. By not moving forward, I was hindering the advancement of God's kingdom in my sphere of influence. I was not allowing the work of God in my life be an encouragement and a source of hope to others who feel stuck in sin.

"Forty", by U2, expresses this journey and the angst of many who have not had the breakthrough they long for. Psalm 40 voices this same longing, but there is power in song to penetrate the deeper levels of your heart. This is a good song to sing to God and to your own soul.

Forty (How Long)
© U2 1983

I waited patiently for the Lord
He inclined and heard my cry
He brought me up out of the pit
Out of the miry clay

I will sing, sing a new song
I will sing, sing a new song

How long to sing this song?
How long to sing this song?
How long, how long
How long, how long to sing this song?

He set my feet upon a rock
And made my footsteps firm
Many will see
Many will see and fear

I will sing, sing a new song
I will sing, sing a new song
I will sing, sing a new song
I will sing, sing a new song

How long to sing this song?

How long to sing this song?

How long, how long

How long, how long to sing this song?

"Forty" speaks of faith in the new song and the tension of waiting to receive it. It is important to sustain your hope by always reminding yourself that victory is sure. This song is not just about personal rescue but about others seeing your redemption and marveling at what God has done.

How is This Book Different?

I wrote this book for the many people who have given up, who have assumed it will take a miracle to deliver them. We may muster up the courage to throw ourselves at a preacher who promises relief through renunciations, prayers, accountability groups, etc., but these tools are like lottery tickets to the poor man. Some find freedom through them, but very, very few.

Along the same lines, many singles feel that marriage will enable them to conquer addiction. Don't count on it. As we go over some of the reasons for our struggles, you will see that many times marriage only makes them worse.

This book is different because in it I look at several doors that may have been opened to addiction and how to close them. At the same time, the primary goal of this book is to open you up to more of what God has for you. Freedom from any sin is insignificant if it is not accompanied by a greater awareness of God's love and plan for you.

My Story

The addiction I battled, pornography, was introduced to me as a child. I remember being elementary school age when my friends and I found *Playboy* Magazines in a dresser drawer. Around the same time a baby sitter showed me how to find the scrambled *Playboy* channel on cable. If I watched closely, I could decipher the images. By middle school, this late night entertainment became my silent partner.

During my freshman year of high school, I gave my life to Christ and thought my habit would end. Instead, it accompanied me into my marriage and work on staff with Campus Crusade. You can imagine my shame: I am leading others in the ways of Christ, but I am not experiencing its truths in my life.

On top of this think through how we, as the Christian community, deal with addiction.

- **Self-Will:** Wow, you need to stop. We need to ask you to step down. You cannot do anything for God while you are struggling with that.

- **Accountability:** Let's get you with some of people who also struggle, so you can share together about problems that none of you know how to deal with. Or, we can put you with people who don't struggle so they can shame you about your issues.

- **Disciplines:** Garbage in; garbage out. You need to spend more time with God. Spend more time in prayer and reading the Bible. Have you tried fasting about it?

- **Faith:** Your problem is you don't believe God can heal you.

- **Spiritual Warfare:** You are under spiritual attack. Take authority over those demons and tell them to leave.

- **Counseling:** Go meet with your pastor or some professional so that they can help you get to know why you struggle. At the very least, read some books. If you really knew yourself, you wouldn't struggle.

The primary reason these suggestions fail is that the focus is on the wrong outcome. While you are so worried about your behavior, God is desperately after your heart.

The secondary reason these suggestions fail is because they are offered piece-meal. None of the suggestions are wrong, but when they are viewed apart from how they work together, they become some secret formula instead of tools drawing you to more of God.

Finally, since these suggestions rarely work but are so commonly endorsed, those struggling in addictions shame themselves for not experiencing the freedom promised in Scripture. They believe victorious Christian living is something denied to them.

Will I Live With This Forever?

I grew up with feet problems–painful, stinky feet problems so bad I had to go to a special doctor. He gave me cream to put on my feet each night. And, every night for 10 years I had sticky, gross sheets due to this treatment.

He gave my issue a name, Atopic Eczema. This special name gave legitimacy to the disease and kept it abstract. He believed the disease came from an allergic reaction to the glue in Nike shoes. I don't remember owning a pair of Nike shoes because of this diagnosis. Filling out the forms for high school sports, I had to inform them I was allergic to the glue from Nike shoes and therefore sentenced to wear Pony's – not the cool swoosh, but the dorky check.

The doctor must have also recommended keeping water away from my feet, because my mom decided to put plastic sandwich baggies on them. In retrospect, it was no surprised this made my condition worse.

Since these measures didn't alleviate the problem, all shoes became suspect, and I was downgraded to sandals. There were no Birkenstocks or Tevas then, so I had to wear thin-strapped sandals. I remember waiting in the cafeteria line in second grade and older kids making fun of my "girl shoes".

I often wondered what was wrong with me. Other people didn't have these problems. I began to feel my condition was evidence I was inherently flawed. I felt the need to hide for fear if others saw the real me, they wouldn't like me. I hated myself.

During college I saw a commercial for Micatin, which showed a close up of a man's foot with fire coming from it and highlighted the soreness between the toes. Those were my symptoms, so I used my dad's can of Micatin, and in a couple of weeks, my feet were feeling better. All these years I had suffered from a bad case of athletc's foot.

I went from elementary school to college plagued with a problem that could have been easily fixed easily by an over-the-counter medication. Worse yet, my dad had a known cure but was talked out of thinking it would work because of the obscure medical name of my condition.

Addiction is like my battle with athlete's foot. Most of us walk around afflicted with an addiction like a fungus, and we don't know how to get rid of it. It bothers us; it affects those around us; but we don't know what to do. We live in shame because we feel it reflects our identity. We believe we are messed up; if people were to find out, they would leave us.

Oftentimes, the solutions we apply exacerbate the problem. In our shame, we hide our sin from others and away from the light of Christ. Jesus has given us the cure. The goal of this book is to help you know how to apply it for complete healing.

How Jesus is the Cure

"Christianity is not a religion; it's a relationship."

Most of us have heard this phrase many times and may have even shared it with our non-Christian friends. But what is that relationship? If we are to take an honest look at how Christians approach their faith, what would it look like? Ask what it means to be a Christian, and you will get a variety of answers: "Go to church," "Pray and read your Bible," "Abstain from bad things like drinking or cursing or sex outside of marriage."

Christians often criticize the Pharisees for their extensive rules, but similarly we have established our own sets of rules for Christian life. Successful Christian living is usually measured by how well we can do what is considered good and avoid what is considered sin. Christianity may be a relationship and not a religion, but most of us do not live that way.

What did Jesus do that made Christianity so different? The Old Testament is characterized by the Law and sacrifices. It follows the basic principles of religion: if you want to be acceptable to God, these are the things you must do. Jesus came to fulfill the Law because we could never do everything necessary to be acceptable.

Nothing you <u>do</u> will ever make you acceptable to God.

As Christians we take Jesus as our Savior and think since He has given us salvation it's now up to us to live in purity. We believe Jesus made it possible for us to live lives acceptable to God, so we establish rules to follow that we think would please Him. This was Paul complaint to the Galatians:

> *"You foolish Galatians! Who has bewitched you? Before your very eyes Jesus Christ was clearly portrayed as crucified. I would like to learn just one thing from you: Did you receive the Spirit by the works of the law, or by believing what you heard? Are you so foolish? After beginning by means of the Spirit, are you now trying to finish by means of the flesh? Have you experienced so much in vain—if it really was in vain? So again I ask, does God give you his Spirit and work miracles among you by the works of the law, or by your believing what you heard?" (Galatians 3:1-5).*

The principle is still true: nothing you *do* will ever make you acceptable to God.

The New Testament is about a new covenant. The old covenant was made with God and Adam. The new covenant is with God and Jesus. In the old covenant, Adam failed to keep the one command and was thus banished from the garden. As descendants of Adam, we are sinful and separated from God. Jesus came and became the last Adam, living a holy and blameless life. Not only did He live in such a way as to stay in God's presence, but He took on the sins of humanity and bore the payment for them. He removed what was keeping us from the presence of God thus fulfilling the old covenant and creating a new one where we are never again separate from God or the benefits of the covenant.

Even though I assume I'm covering over ideas most of you know, for many, these concepts have not made it into practice. The reason why we can do nothing to make ourselves acceptable to God is because it has already been done. Jesus made us acceptable. Reading our Bible and praying will not make us more acceptable. AND, since our sins have been paid for, when we do sin, it does not make us any less acceptable.

This is the biggest lie those who struggle with addiction: you have to do something to get your healing. You, my friend, already have your healing! Our role in this new covenant is not to keep the covenant, but to abide in Jesus – the one with whom the covenant was made. We must transform our thinking in order to live this out.

How Do You Chain an Elephant?

Elephants are the largest land animals and definitely one of the strongest. However these massive animals can be held captive by a simple rope and stake. It is almost unthinkable to think a large elephant can be retained by instruments that an average human can pull out, but it happens and here's why.

At an early age trainers will tie up the young elephant with a rope and stake. The young elephant doesn't like the restriction, but at this time of development, it doesn't have the strength to pull the stake out or break the rope. In fact the more it pulls, the more it hurts the young elephant. Over time the elephant gives up on the rope.

As the elephant grows up, it remembers the pain of pulling on the rope. And, while it could now easily pull the rope out, it never tries. The pain of the past holds the elephant in its current bondage.

This is how most of us are held in addiction. We are more than able to break free, yet the memories of past pain and fear of future pain keep us from really attaining freedom. We may try half-heartedly at breaking free, but as the pain floods back into our memory, we give up.

Addiction is not insurmountable—freedom is attainable. As you read this book, you will see you have all that you need to break free. You can do it. Press on.

2

NOT ABOUT THE ACT

Your Goal in Reading This Book

Let's be honest with each other, our main goal in reading and writing this book is to be completely free from addiction. The dream of being completely free is a fantastic one, which is almost too good to imagine. If we could just remove that one source of shame from our lives, we would feel right with God and man. But God sees it all differently. He is not looking for you to act or not act a certain way. Jesus has already taken care of the sin issue. God cares about the heart (Psalm 51:16-17).

We as Christians don't understand this aspect of God. If you have been a Christian for long, you have been introduced to accountability groups. Listening to the questions in these groups will expose our view of Christianity. The main question they are trying to get to is: "have you fallen into your addiction this week?". All of the other questions are usually focused on things that we feel that would reduce that desire to fall. The goal tends not to be the relationship with Jesus or others, but the corralling of evil desires.

Your sinful act is only an outward expression of something going on in the heart (Luke 6:45). Since sin has been dealt with, God has transformed sin from bringing a curse to bringing His grace by exposing darkened areas of the heart. However, since most of us still see sin as bringing a curse, we don't follow the grace into the real causes that are leading us to the addiction.

What is the Importance of Confession?

You may be protesting that accountability groups give you a place to confess your sins. I agree that they play that role and confession is important, but have you ever thought about why confession is important? So many times in my Christian walk I have been told that without confession there is no forgiveness. "If we confess our sins, He is faithful and just to forgive us our sins and cleanse us of all unrighteousness" (1 John 1:9). The problem is we have already been forgiven (1 John 2:12). And, if that were not the case, we would never have confessed all of our sins completely enough to find true forgiveness.

So, what is the importance of confession? There is an interesting passage in Hosea that I believe brings to light God's desires for confession. It is found in Hosea 2:5–13; 14–23. The book of Hosea is about how God made the prophet go marry a prostitute to symbolize God's love for Israel. This passage shows the rationale of the importance of exposing sin.

Hosea 2:5–13

5 Their mother has been unfaithful and has conceived them in disgrace. She said, 'I will go after my lovers, who give me my food and my water, my wool and my linen, my oil and my drink.'

6 Therefore I will block her path with thornbushes; I will wall her in so that she cannot find her way.

7 She will chase after her lovers but not catch them; she will look for them but not find them. Then she will say, 'I will go back to my husband as at first, for then I was better off than now.'

8 She has not acknowledged that I was the one who gave her the grain, the new wine and oil, who lavished on her the silver and gold—which they used for Baal.

9 "Therefore I will take away my grain when it ripens, and my new wine when it is ready. I will take back my wool and my linen, intended to cover her nakedness.

10 So now I will expose her lewdness before the eyes of her lovers; no one will take her out of my hands.

11 I will stop all her celebrations: her yearly festivals, her New Moons, her Sabbath days—all her appointed feasts.

12 I will ruin her vines and her fig trees, which she said were her pay from her lovers; I will make them a thicket, and wild animals will devour them.

13 I will punish her for the days she burned incense to the Baals; she decked herself with rings and jewelry, and went after her lovers, but me she forgot," declares the LORD.

Israel has been unfaithful going after other things instead of God (v.5). How does God respond? He actively blocks her path to keep her from her lovers; He takes away His provisions for her; and He exposes her lewdness (v. 6, 9-10).

We read this and think we see God's hatred of the sin. "If you are going to treat me this way, than I am going to turn away from you?" But this is not what's going on. God's response is based out of love for Israel. God may sound mad in the section, but as we continue we can see His love and intentions.

Hosea 2:14-23

14 "Therefore I am now going to allure her; I will lead her into the desert and speak tenderly to her.

15 There I will give her back her vineyards, and will make the Valley of Achor a door of hope. There she will sing as in the days of her youth, as in the day she came up out of Egypt.

16 "In that day," declares the LORD, "you will call me 'my husband'; you will no longer call me 'my master.'

17 I will remove the names of the Baals from her lips; no longer will their names be invoked.

18 In that day I will make a covenant for them with the beasts of the field and the birds of the air and the creatures that move along the ground. Bow and sword and battle I will abolish from the land, so that all may lie down in safety.

19 I will betroth you to me forever; I will betroth you in righteousness and justice, in love and compassion.

20 I will betroth you in faithfulness, and you will acknowledge the LORD.

21 "In that day I will respond," declares the LORD— "I will respond to the skies, and they will respond to the earth;

22 and the earth will respond to the grain, the new wine and oil, and they will respond to Jezreel.

23 I will plant her for myself in the land; I will show my love to the one I called 'Not my loved one.' I will say to those called 'Not my people,' 'You are my people'; and they will say, 'You are my God.'"

God starts to allure and speak tenderly to Israel (v. 14). Israel could not receive God's love for her while she was still holding on to other lovers. Therefore God removed His blessing, not as a form of punishment, but in an attempt to make her feel her weakness without Him. He knew her attachment to these other lovers would hinder her from receiving the full measure of His love, and He loved her too much to leave her sin hidden.

Therefore once God exposes Israel's sin and gets her to a place of weakness, He tries to win back her affection. He allures her. He speaks tenderly to her. He starts to give back that which He withheld. It is amazing to see God as such a jealous lover that He fights for His bride, yet after fighting He does not assume her love. He humbly seeks to win her favor. The God, who can do anything He wants, does not presume that we will respond, but seeks to make us want Him by courting us.

The story becomes even more incredible. Before the relationship was a servant/master. Now, it is one of lovers—a husband/wife (v. 16, 23). Do you see? This is God's plan. He wants intimate lovers, but sin hinders our view of Him and the best we can see the relationship being is servant/master. We confess our sins, not for the forgiveness. We confess our sins in order to walk out our forgiveness. Because I know that I am forgiven, I can expose my sins to the light of His love to see He does not hold hatred or disappointment in me, but love and forgiveness.

Leaving our sins hidden in darkness exposes lies we believe about God's forgiveness–that we have gone beyond His grace or He will not take care of me. We are not some sort of project that we have to be corrected or supervised in order to gain His favor. He loves us because He delights in us. We bring Him joy.

Although sin saddens God's heart, it is not because it angers Him – the cross dealt with that. Sin saddens Him because He loves us so much He wants us to experience all of the joy in His heart for us. Stop worrying about your ministry or what others may think of you. Confess your sins so that you may run in the delight of God's extravagant love for you.

Why It is Important Not to Focus on the Act

God wants so much more for you than merely freedom from sin. All sin is just symptoms of deeper issues going on. Even if you are able to contain the act, some other sin will pop up in another area of your life if the heart is not addressed. That is why you see alcoholics trading alcohol for anger or overeaters trading food for exercise.

Maturity is not measured by outward expressions. Maturity in the Lord happens in the heart. Remember God's rebuke to Samuel:

But the LORD said to Samuel, "Do not consider his appearance or his height, for I have rejected him. The LORD does not look at the things man looks at. Man looks at the outward appearance, but the LORD looks at the heart." – 1 Samuel 16:7

Focusing on the sin also hinders you from celebrating the successes you do have. For instance, say you feel God is leading you to have regular time reading the Bible. You rearrange your schedule and work in time to read. You may even regularly spent time for several weeks. And yet, if your main goal is freedom from addiction, no joy can be taken from your success if you don't see improvement in your behavior. Instead you will look back at those few months of discipline and question God's faithfulness. While that one discipline will more than likely not "do the trick," it will prepare your heart to experience more of God that can get you more in a place to find the healing you are after.

Focusing on the act reduces the joy of growth. But, maturity in Christ is a growth process not a bunch of external expressions. "Perseverance must finish its work so that you may be mature and complete, not lacking anything" (James 1:4).

3

NOT A ONE-TRICK ANSWER

Some People Find Freedom Through a One-Trick Answer

In my freshman year of high school, I went to a Christian concert where t-shirts were for sale that had "Love God, Hate Sin" in large print on the back. Before the show I talked to my friends about the craziness of someone wearing that in public. After the concert my heart was changed, and I was the proud owner of that "crazy" shirt, which I boldly wore to school the next day. My conversion may not have been outwardly drastic, but my devotion to the Lord was strong. Ever since that night I placed my faith in Jesus, I have loved Him dearly.

Pornography was that ugly blemish always restricting my devotion to Jesus by adding fears of failure and of exposure. Throughout high school and college I would hear speakers share of their personal experiences coming out of addiction. Some would share how after that moment of salvation, they never picked up another magazine. Some would tell of their change of priorities where they would now pick up the Bible instead of the remote. I would also hear some tell of their experience of being delivered from demonic oppression and never go back to that lifestyle again. Each time I heard them speak, I would wonder if this was the moment of freedom for me. Was this the magic formula I had been looking for?

Each time this new trick did not work, questions arose in my head that maybe something was wrong with me. Everyone else seems to be getting it. Why am I being left out? The whole thing felt unfair; it felt as if God was not holding on to His part of the deal.

Anyone Who Continues to Sin

To make matters worse, there was the verse in 1 John that seemed to also point to something being wrong.

"No one who lives in him keeps on sinning. No one who continues to sin has either seen him or known him." — *1 John 3:6*

Are you kidding me? Is this really true? Am I to believe that I really don't know God since I am still carrying around this sin?

Whenever you come to a passage of Scripture you don't understand, it is best to start by trying to understand the context. This passage is surrounded by expressions of love toward us from the Father, Son, and Holy Spirit. It is in the context of this love for us, John makes the comment about us not knowing God.

This started to make more sense to me as I thought about my marriage. Now, I am in love with my wife, and I really don't know how to love anyone else more. Even so, there are times she asks me to do some things that in the heat of the moment cause anger and frustration to rise in my heart. These feelings are not evidences that I really don't love my wife; they just show that I am not living in the full awareness of that love. It is in these moments that God gives me a glimpse to an area in my heart that has also not truly seen or experienced the fullness of love.

"This is how we know what love is: Jesus Christ laid down his life for us. And we ought to lay down our lives for our brothers." — *1 John 3:16*

John, in his inspired wisdom, is helping us to see sin as a tool of growth in the Lord. Before he looks at sin, he reminds us of the great love of God our Father. In the middle, he reminds us of the great expression of the love of God the Son. And at the end, he reminds us of the gentle reminders of love from God the Spirit. Bathed in love, John can have us look at sin without the discouragement of condemnation.

What is John trying to say? Don't look at sin as something you need to remove solely on your own! If you are continuing to sin, then there is something about God's love that has not transformed that area. Your struggle with addiction is an open invitation to ask Holy Spirit what part of God's love you are missing. It is not saying you don't know Him at all; there is just something that has been tainted.

I used to live where there were mountains all around. During the sunrises and sunsets, the mountains would block the light and colors. While in the full light of day, there were no shadows. Since the sun is always moving, shadows would come and go. God works in similar ways. He is moving the light of His presence around in our lives to show us areas still untouched by His love. We are not to shrink back in shame when we are exposed. We are to be reminded of His complete love for us, and rejoice at the exposure knowing complete healing is coming.

We must bring things out of the darkness for the impurities of our lives to be burned away. This cleansing process leads us to confidence before God because we have opened ourselves to His correction and felt completely loved. As we move out from that experience, we know we are children of God, and we can ask anything from our Father who has moved every obstacle for us to experience the fullness of His affection for us.

"Dear friends, if our hearts do not condemn us, we have confidence before God and receive from him anything we

ask, because we obey his commands and do what pleases him." — 1 John 3:21-22

Lord, Don't Give Us What We Deserve

As Holy Spirit starts to expose these areas in our lives, there is a temptation to pray, "Lord, don't give us what we deserve." What we mean with this request is, "Lord, we see sin in our own lives, and we know that You are holy. Since Your justice demands punishment, please don't punish us." This sounds humble and contrite, but it is a lie from the enemy to keep us from having confidence as we approach God.

Here is what I mean. In your mind's eye, picture Calvary. Who is on the cross? Jesus. What was He doing there? He was paying for the penalty for our sins. How much of that penalty did He pay for? He paid for all of it. I'm sorry for the simple logic, but too many Christians believe there is still punishment for our sins. There is no more judgment left for us. When we placed our lives in Christ, we exchanged our lives for His. All of the negative behaviors, thoughts, and attitudes were placed with Christ on the cross. They are forever taken care of. Therefore, we have no more fear of condemnation or judgment of sins (Romans 8:1). We can now boldly enter the throne room of God with confidence because we are now hidden in Christ (Hebrews 4:16).

AND, all of the blessings that are for Christ are also bestowed on us. We are blessed in the heavenly realms with every spiritual blessing in Christ (Ephesians 1:3). Now then, what do we, who are in Christ, deserve? We deserve all rights and privileges that are set aside for the sons and daughters of promise. He who has given us His only Son, will He not also freely give us all things? (Romans 8:32)!!!

How much does this thought change how you approach God? We can come with confidence knowing that we have what we ask. We can now take our request to God saying, "Lord, give me what I deserve. Those rights and privileges attributed to me at the Cross, I want them.

For many of you, your views of God and self are strongly opposing this concept. It doesn't feel right. You are still feeling like the prodigal son on his way home: "I'm not even worthy of being called His son." The kingdom of God is like the father who puts sandals on your feet, a robe on your back, and a ring on your finger. Which will make God happier: to refuse His gifts because you feel unworthy, or to eager pursue what He wants to give you?

You have been adopted into the family of God. You have all the rights and privileges of a legitimate son and daughter. You are a new creation. Eagerly desire what God eagerly wants you to have.

God is Not Looking for Formulas but Relationships

Above all else, God wants us to have an intimate friendship with Him, and He uses everything that comes at us as an invitation for us to move closer to Him. This is one of the purposes of considering trials pure joy (James 1:2). Therefore don't get caught up with mastery over addiction; focus on what God is trying to tell you in the midst of it. The Pharisees strived to be holy and got the strongest rebukes from Jesus because they lost focus on God's ultimate goal. Purity is awesome; intimacy is best. If you perfect the latter, failures at the former are overlooked. That is why David can commit adultery and murder and still be called a man after God's own heart.

Still holiness is important, and for many of us, loving God more hasn't changed our behavior. The truth is some people do win the lottery. There are some who make that one change and God removes from them the burden of whatever was their addiction. The rest of us have to struggle for even minor victories. He has us all on different paths. Just have faith that all paths that lead to more of God's love and perfection in God's love will also lead to holiness. The next several chapters will dive into what it practically looks like to see more of God's love in your life.

4

BROKEN FOUNDATIONS

We Love God Because He First Loved Us

Have you ever thought you just did not love God enough? Maybe that is why God has not removed the addiction from your life. Well, don't let it get you down because we can all love God more. We can only love God to the measure that we ourselves have been loved or to the extent that we understand His love for us. Remember the woman who barges in the dinner party to bathe Jesus' feet with tears? Jesus said the she loves much because she had experienced much of God's love and forgiveness (Luke 7:36-50).

We love because He first loved us. If you want to love God more, then you need to first receive more of His love. When we place all of our focus on ourselves to generate the loving feelings for God, it will lead to striving and religion—trying to earn God's favor.

What then keeps us from God's love? First of all, it is not God. He has bent over backwards to show us that He loves us. Sending His Son to die on the cross is a huge sign. "He who did not spare his own Son, but gave him up for us all—how will he not also, along with him, graciously give us all things?" (Romans 8:32)

While it is true that no one seeks God without the Father drawing them, it is just as true that no one would blatantly reject the love of Christ if they really knew it. Therefore misinterpretations of events and lies in our hearts block our view of His love. Knowing that they were deceived, Jesus was able to say from the cross, "Father forgive them for they know not what they are doing" (Luke 23:34). When we really know in our hearts the love of God, we would come running, weeping, and rejoicing into the arms of our Father.

This is why sin management does not get at the true issue of the sin. The true root is a misunderstanding of God and yourself. This is also why God has gone through so much trouble to do away with the punishment of sin. He knew that if we were so worried about getting punished we would be too focused on the wrong thing. Since we know that we have no condemnation in Christ Jesus, we can freely explore our hearts to unearth these misinterpretations and lies we believe about God and ourselves.

How Lies Keep Us From God

There can be multiple lies that each of us believe, but I will walk through a typical one for many. Many people grew up in a busy family where your parents did not have much free time to play with you. Or, maybe your parents were divorced limiting your time with one or both of them. Whatever the cause, many people have developed the lie: "you are not important enough for those you care about to make time for you."

In other words, you live life as if you are unworthy or you don't measure up. Therefore you live your life either trying to prove to others and yourself that you actually do measure up by your efforts and striving, or you give in and stop trying altogether taking on a "why bother" attitude on life.

As a Christian you decide to accept Jesus as your Lord and Savior. For the first time in your life you start to receive a different interpretation about yourself. Then trials hit and your mind is flooded with those same feeling you had before. In your pain you go back to the patterns that have always made sense to you. You say, "God is so good and kind that He wants everyone to go to heaven, but now that I have received Him, He does not have time for me. There are more important people for Him to attend to." And then, you go back to same patterns of living. Either you try to earn God's favor in order to get His attention, or you give up because God does not have time for you anyway. Both ways are motivated by a fear of rejection. Either, "I feel rejected, so I will try harder at pleasing Him." Or, "I will always be rejected, so I will not try too hard or care too much because the pain is too great." Can you see how lies are keeping us from going to God? Can you see why lies are keeping us from understanding the love of Christ?

We need to see loving God as we do tithing. We give God a portion of our wages as an act of thankfulness for the provisions that He gave us. If He did not give us the money, we would have nothing to give back to Him. Loving God is the same. We can only love God with the love we have first received from Him.

If you want to love God more, start asking Him to show you what lies you believe that are keeping you from receiving what He so willingly wants to give.

How Misinterpretations Work

"And we know that in all things God works for the good of those who love him, who have been called according to his purpose." — Romans 8:28

Lies enter your way of thinking through many doors. Sometimes you are seemingly born with them. Sometimes you learn them from your parents. Other times events in your life lead you into an incorrect understanding of the world and God. For now I'll focus on this last potential door.

For the past few years, with the nationwide unemployment rate ranging between 9 - 10% and an economic recession, many people are questioning the goodness of God for them. Homes are being foreclosed and people are being laid off. As people struggle to make ends meet, they may show an outward dependence on God, but inwardly they believe God has forgotten them. We would never let our loved one go through these hardships, so God must not really love us. We reason that maybe God only cares about our salvation, so we are on our own for the rest of our lives.

This is an example that many can relate to since it is portrayed nightly on the news, but there are an infinite variety of events that could move you. Life is full of events that make you question the existence of God and His goodness. Think through any of these potential circumstances:

- others get promoted before you
- you wreck your car
- a friend slanders you behind your back
- you have a miscarriage
- your spouse leaves you
- your child dies before you do
- you are diagnosed with cancer

Each of these events appears bad. Yes, I said, "appears". Only God has the right to interpret the events of our lives. If we chose to interpret them without Him, we will allow lies to take root in our hearts. Let's take for example something as common as having a miscarriage (I've heard that 20% of pregnancies end in a miscarriage).

What goes through the mind of a young woman when her she has miscarried? She suffers tremendous grief, as it is a loss of a child. One of the first things she will consider is whether she had done something wrong. Did she not take the right vitamins or was she not eating right? But, also just as quick, she will question God about why He took her child. He was ultimately in control. He can do whatever He wants. He could have saved her baby? But, He chose not to. Can you see how easy it is for the logic to go there?

Now she has put herself in the place of receiving any of these lies:

- God does not want me to have a child.
- He thinks I would not have been a good mom.
- I am too selfish to have a child.
- I have messed up too much to get anything from God.
- God loves the world, but He does not love me.
- My husband would be better off with someone else.
- I am worthless.
- Nobody would miss me if I was gone.

John 11 tells the story of the death of Lazarus. This is a very intriguing account with Jesus. First of all, He hears that His friend, Lazarus, is sick. Then He waits a couple days before going to him. In verse 15, He says that He was glad that He was not there before Lazarus died.

When He strolls into town, Lazarus' sisters have separate encounters with Jesus. Both say to Him that if He had been there Lazarus would not have died. They both interpreted Lazarus' death as something bad. Jesus, as we already saw in verse 15, interpreted the event differently. He was going to raise Lazarus from the dead.

Your story may not have the same ending. Your loved one may not be given back to you. Your sickness may end in death. However, God does say that He will work for the good for those who love Him. If you are a believer and tragedy comes your way, you have every right to go to God and ask for His interpretation. "If any of you lacks wisdom, he should ask God, who gives generously" (James 1:5). The only way to avoid the lies and to live in the truth is to allow God to interpret the events of your life. Hold fast to the truth that God works all things for good!

If you are having trouble believing God's goodness because of an event in your life, pray through the heart of our loving Father. He is the one who takes all that is bad and makes it good for His people (Isaiah 61:7). My friend, God loves you!

How Can God Make Good Out of This?

I know some people have gone through some intensely painful events. There is so much evil in the world, and you could very well have been the brunt of more than your share. I know the scandals of some youth group leaders toward students with whom they work. I know relatives sometimes abuse their familial trust to young kids who are unable to comprehend what is happening. I know some spouses are blatantly hateful with their words and actions. Am I saying that your interpretations of those events are incorrect?

If you cannot look back on those events without fear and anger, then yes.

Have you ever thought how Joseph must have felt through the Christmas story (Matthew 1:18-25)? He is engaged to be married to a teenage girl who surprisingly turns up pregnant. A virgin birth was no more believable in his time than it would be now. He may not have had the wonders of modern science, but he must have known how babies were created. How devastating this must have been for him. The Bible says Joseph wanted to do what was right, but there was also disgrace and personal sorrow that went with his fiancé being pregnant. We get a hint that this shame was placed on the family as the Jews slap a remark on Jesus insinuating that He was an illegitimate child (John 8:41).

In God's mercy He sends Joseph an angel to encourage him that Mary was telling the truth about her carrying the Christ-child. We need to remember this. In our own wisdom the things of God will not make sense to us. We need to go to Him to allow Jesus to interpret our circumstances. Only then will we have the wisdom to make it through life.

Have you ever thought of how Bathsheba felt in her story (2 Samuel 11:1 – 12:24)? Here you are going about life and one day, out of the blue, you are called into the King's presence. He rapes you and sends you home. Your husband is off at war. You may have your family with you, but what kind of condolences would you get? He's the King. You're just a woman.

Later you find out your pregnant. You hear rumors that your husband is being brought in from war. You have to know that the purposes of these events because the King would not risk having you tell your husband what happened. Each night you wait for your husband to come home, and he doesn't show.

You had just experienced the humiliation of being the object of one man's lust and then thrown aside when he was finished. Now the one man who is supposed to love and protect you won't come to your side. What would he do when he finds out your pregnant? Thoughts of raising a child alone start to form in your mind. What would you think about God, yourself, or God's view of you?

Then on top of the depression that must have already been setting in, your husband is killed at war. The reason of his death you would assuredly find out at some point was the man who caused all of your pain. Remember Nathan's rebuke of David portrayed Bathsheba as the innocent lamb stolen from the love of another and sacrificed for the portrayer's pleasure. Bathsheba was stolen from one who loved her.

Would God ever step in and make good come out of this? Most assuredly He does. Bathsheba is eventually brought into the lineage of the coming Christ. It is her son Solomon that replaces David on the throne. Her son is the one who is king during the grandest time of Israel's history.

We are not to look at the painful events and say God caused them. But, we must trust the power of our Almighty Creator God to be able to take those evil circumstances and create something exponentially greater than the evil that was bestowed.

Whatever painful circumstances you have endured, take them to Jesus. Allow Him to interpret them for you. The truth of any circumstance is only what Jesus says is true about it.

Finding Joy in Every Circumstance

The lies we believe and the misinterpretations of events in our lives are the two keys of fully unraveling what's keeping us from the love of the Father. Notice it is not addiction. Addiction is just a symptom revealing the deeper sickness. We need to look beyond the pain to the joy God has in store for us.

In Hebrews 12:2 we are commanded to be continually "looking unto Jesus, the author and finisher of our faith, who for the joy that was set before Him endured the cross, despising the shame, and has sat down at the right hand of the throne of God." It would have been devastating if Jesus went to the cross and could only see the pain and the suffering of what lay ahead. This verse says that it was for the joy that was set before Him that He endured the cross. He had hope of an ending that made the present not only endurable but worth it. We are to do the same.

By looking to Jesus instead of our circumstances, we will learn to experience joy in the midst of any situation. Things don't have to be going well or to have gone well for us to experience joy because joy does not come from the events of our lives. Joy comes from the work of Holy Spirit in us and the future set before us. He is constantly engineering our lives to take us to the most beneficial place. Evil hits, which seemingly moves us off track, but God just redesigns the track to take us to an even better plan than we were already given. Whenever we turn our eyes off Jesus, we stifle the work of Holy Spirit and miss the opportunity to hear how God will make good out of it.

This is why we are to give thanks in everything (1 Thessalonians 5:18). Thanksgiving is an act of faith that God will work all things out for our good. It is an overflow of living by the Spirit (Ephesians 5:18-20). By always thanking God for everything, we refocus our eyes on the One who loves us and is taking us through to the other side.

How Can We Thank God for Difficult Events

Several years ago now, my wife and I went though the most difficult time in our marriage. She found out that my struggle with pornography was not over as I was leading her to believe. It was a very painful and strenuous time for us, and it did not look like we were going to make through. Our lives were thrown upside down, and we were being painfully humbled. During two weeks that we were living apart I remember going to God with my pain and expressing my sense of hopelessness. While praying I remembered the command to thank God for everything. I did not want to. My whole world was collapsing. How could I ever thank God for something as terrible as that?

I remembered Romans 8:28 and 1 Thessalonians 5:18. Was I going to trust God or believe what the circumstances were leading me to believe? Although I did not feel like it could work out for good, I decided to trust God and hold onto His promise. I thanked God for taking me through that very difficult and painful time as an act of trust that He would work it out for the good. Thankfully, now I can look back and see many wonderful things God gave to us through that time. And, I trust more good is still going to come through it.

By thanking God in the midst of circumstances that seem awful, we are saying to God, "God, I don't see You in this, but I trust You know what You are doing and can make this good." And, by saying this we open ourselves up to hear what Jesus is doing.

5

REPAIRING THE HEART

Overview of Healing

Up to this point I have set the stage of complete freedom to be more than stopping the sinful behavior. This is necessary to create the lasting motivation to properly go through the practical steps of getting clean. Focus on the act brings discouragement at every "failure." Focus on growing in Christ sees everything as an opportunity of growth and intimacy.

We have been given everything we need for life and godliness through our knowledge of Jesus (2 Peter 1:3). We need to keep that in focus or else we will not be free. Peter said he always reminds believers of these things, even if they know them already (2 Peter 1:12-13). It is essential not to lose focus of why we need the healing from addiction.

With that said, there are some practical steps that can help this process along. First, look at this Belief-Behavior Cycle from Restoring the Foundations Ministry. What it represents is that we all have experiences that define our beliefs. Our beliefs set our expectations, which influence our behaviors. Our behaviors then create experiences that solidify the beliefs we have already come to believe.

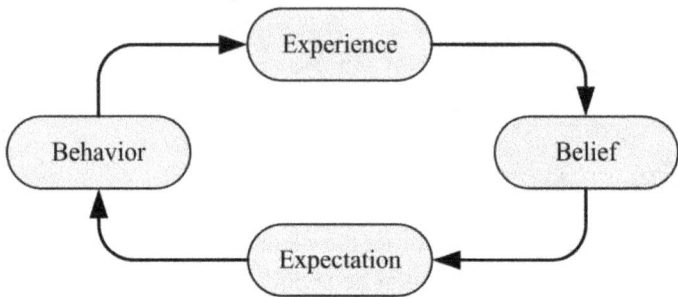

Belief-Behavior Cycle

This is why focusing on just the behavior is often fruitless because the underlying beliefs motivating that behavior is still in place. It is also helps to understand why some people can have one experience to break this cycle. It is all about correcting those wrong beliefs.

We will correct these wrong beliefs by correcting four areas of entry:

1. Generational Sins

2. Wrong Beliefs

3. Misinterpreted Past

4. Evil Spirits

Step 1: Our Parents' Sins Hamstring Our Success

This may be an interesting first step, but it is foundational. Whether we like it or not, we have been given blessings and curses from our parents. They set the stage for our lives before we even have a choice for ourselves. We are not bound to them, but they put pressure on us to behave the same way they did, either for God or against Him. Dealing with these blessings and curses can make future work much easier.

I, the LORD your God, am a jealous God, punishing the children for the sin of the fathers to the third and fourth generation of those who hate me, but showing love to a thousand {generations} of those who love me and keep my commandments. – Exodus 20:5-6

Embedded within the first commandment is this foundational principle of God. Your sin brings a curse to you and your children. Your righteousness brings blessings to you and your children. There is something within the makeup of man and the spiritual realm where these curses and blessings are past down. This is a great encouragement that we can build off the successes of those who have gone before us, but almost in order to get it in place, there are some negative attributes that are also passed.

Before we go any further with the sins, I want to highlight the good that comes from this. It is this principle that Paul draws on in Romans 5 as he links Jesus to Adam.

"Consequently, just as the result of one trespass was condemnation for all men, so also the result of one act of righteousness was justification that brings life for all men." – Romans 5:18

How can we be held accountable for Adam's sin? How can Jesus' death bring life for all men? It is through the doors created with this principle. Also notice which is stronger. Jesus righteousness overcame the curse of Adam's sin. Also the curses from Exodus 20 go down the line to the third and fourth generation, but the blessings follow to a thousand generations.

While the sins of our parents do open doors in our lives to curses, please remember that the heart of our heavenly Father is to bless you. This is the encouragement the writer of Hebrews gives regarding why faith is important: God rewards those that seek Him (Hebrews 11:6).

Those Curses Do Not Have to Hinder Us

"Christ redeemed us from the curse of the law by becoming a curse for us, for it is written: 'Cursed is everyone who is hung on a tree.'" – Galatians 3:13

We do not need to live with the effects of any curse on our lives. They have all been done away with on the cross. But just with salvation, we need to apply it to our lives.

"But if they will confess their sins and the sins of their fathers… then when their uncircumcised hearts are humbled and they pay for their sin, I will remember my covenant with Jacob and my covenant with Isaac and my covenant with Abraham, and I will remember the land." – Leviticus 26:40-42

Remember the prayers of Nehemiah when he heard that the walls of Jerusalem were in rubble? He confesses the sins of Israel and includes himself in those prayers. The removal of the curse is found in the confession of sins. Leviticus lays out this process of tapping into God's heart in the matter: Come into agreement with me about these things. Call sin, sin. Then turn from them. Remember the curses are only there to lead you back to the loving arms of the Father.

Take a sheet of paper and ask God to show you all the sins of your parents or others in your generational line. The point of this is not to get mad at your parents; it is tool for freedom. As you are praying, write down everything that comes to mind, even the ones that you question if they are true. You are not holding people accountable for their stuff; you are just trying to get as much freedom for yourself as you can get.

For each one of these things, confess them for your parents, yourself, and others in your family line that God brings to mind. Choose to forgive them for the sin, the consequences in your life, and the curses that were passed to you. Forgiveness is extremely important to God and to your healing, so make sure you release them from any anger you hold.

Ask the Lord to forgive you for any involvement you have had in this sin, and thank God for His forgiveness. Renounce the sin and the curses of the sin. Claim the promise that Jesus became the curse for you (Galatians 3:13). Finally, receive God's freedom from this sin and the resulting curses by faith.

In summary:
- Confess
- Forgive Parents
- Forgive Self
- Receive Forgiveness
- Renounce Sin
- Receive Freedom

Finding Freedom by Breaking Curses Passed Down

While working with college students, my wife and I were introduced to a student who lived under extreme addictions. She had gotten drunk every night since she was 16 and had a habit of self-mutilation. One of the things we found out through helping her was her grandmother's devotion to witchcraft. She went through this process of confessing her grandmother's sin and breaking the curses that were passed down and spoken over her. It was not long after this that drinking and self-mutilation no longer had any hold on her.

I chose this example, because we are more open to accept the effects of witchcraft passing down issues to later generations. But we must not limit our view to only these over-the-top examples. Anger, depression, hypochondria, workaholic, promiscuity, etc. can all just as easily pass down curses. There is a simple example in the Bible where Isaac displayed a similar sin to that of his father, Abraham, of lying about his wife (Genesis 12:11-13; 20:2, 26:7). Root out all possible doors evil may claim on your life and break the hold they have.

Step 2: Lies Keep Us from Experiencing All God Has for Us

"We act out what we believe. Not what we know." –
Vickie Arruda

I love this quote because it so powerfully states the need for us to think rightly. It also shows how we as Christians can memorize plenty of Scriptures and still be stuck in sin. It is drastically important for us to take the truths of God and get them to the point of deeply held beliefs.

As those who struggle with addictions, there is a common belief that you have messed up so badly that you have missed God's best for you. You may feel like this is true, but it is not. You cannot find this in Scripture. In fact you find just the opposite. The Scripture is full of examples that you cannot get so far from God that He cannot bring you back: Jonah, Moses, David, Paul, Mark, etc.

Think about Mark. Here is the young believer that was at the root of the split of the first missionary pair. Mark abandons Paul and Barnabas during their first missionary trip. As Paul and Barnabas are making plans for their second trip, Barnabas wants to give Mark another chance. Paul is adamant this was not going to happen. The disagreement is so deep that Barnabas takes Mark leaving Paul to pair up with Silas (Acts 15:26-40).

Imagine the pain that could have caused Mark. You know younger believers see those spiritual fathers as speaking the very words of God. Paul had basically said that Mark was an unfaithful believer and not good enough to risk another chance. We are not shown whether this lie actually took root within Mark, but you can see formative events that would have led to it.

Thankfully for all of us, Barnabas put his time and heart within this young believer. Those remarks and actions from Paul could have sidelined this minister of the Gospel for the rest of his life. But, the lie that Mark had messed up so badly that God could not use him was going to be proved untrue later in life. Not only does Mark write one of the four Gospels that God chose to give us, Paul also calls for Mark in his time of imprisonment in Rome because "he was helpful to his ministry" (2 Timothy 4:11).

Working through these lies is how we transform our minds and take every thought captive. If we act out of what we believe, we need to make sure what we believe is what God says is true. When we find ourselves struggling to live in accordance with Scripture, ask God to reveal the lies you are believing. Most of the time you are believing multiple lies. Don't let this discourage you. Allow it to give you hope for a greater experience with Jesus ahead.

This idea has had the greatest impact on my own healing and relationship with God. There were so many lies that I was living under. They were sabotaging what God desired to accomplish through me. I could not follow through with the steps He laid out for my healing or for ministry because deep down I had incorrect views of God and myself.

For instance, I believed that if people found out the real me, they would leave me. Therefore I allowed my pain and struggles to remain hidden for fear of being abandoned by those I cared about. I also lived out of performance to what I thought would get me the affection I desired from others. I never let the real me out, which led me to the point I didn't even know the real me. This showed itself each time I took personality tests – I always came out with a different result.

Fearing that the real me would cause others to leave me also kept me from God because I believed I also needed to perform for Him and that He had made a mistake in making me the way I was. This also made it difficult for me to confess sin. In the context of that lie I felt it was another way to feel rejected by God. "O God, here is another example that the real me is messed up. I don't know how long You will keep putting up with me. Help me to be someone different."

Here is the truth that I needed to believe: God made the real me, and when people get to know the real me they would be drawn to me. I didn't need God make me into someone else; my real me was better than I knew. This truth was too good to believe.

I also believed a lie that one of my true identities was I was a failure. I could do nothing right. This supported my reasoning to hide what I thought was my real self. I also hid from any responsibilities that would bring attention to me. I would say things that sounded humble, "I want to be the person that helps the one ultimately responsible to accomplish their goals." Let me be second in command – runner-up – VP. My real reason for this statement was it would allow me to feel important through someone else's success and not get the blame when things went wrong. I did not want to be proven a failure again.

This also affected how I read the Bible. I read that I was more than overcomer or created to do good works, but I did not feel they were really true for me. God called me a son, but I felt I was just sneaking in the back door. All my spiritual activity was based out of trying to correct this idea that I was a failure, but every time I missed the mark, I would retreat into negative self-talk and destructive thinking.

The truth was I *am* an overcomer (Romans 8:37). I *can do* all things through Christ who strengthens me (Philippians 4:13). God *does bless* the works of my hands (Deuteronomy 2:7). I needed to believe that God's desire to bless me was greater than my ability to fail. And, when I did not experience the success I hoped for, it was not to condemn me as a failure.

I needed to confess these lies as sin. Thank God for His forgiveness. Renounce them. Then ask God what He said was true. Once God gave me these truths, I prayed through them every day until I felt as if they were true. And, when I came to instances where I had a choice of which truth to live out of, I would actively chose to live out of what God said by faith.

Step 3: Your Misinterpreted Past Keeps You from Stepping Out Again

The lies we believe often feel true because the events in our lives seem to support them. Whenever we come to a circumstance when we cannot see God's truths being real, we need to go to Him to help us see from His perspective. His perspective diffuses the lies to make way for us to receive the truth.

Several years ago, I going through a very difficult time that was affecting my work, home life, and hope for the future. It was another event where I was being tempted to believe again I was a failure. I did not see God blessing the work of my hands, and it appeared that someone close to me was starting to reject me. I was in the crisis of belief. Would I choose to believe what God said about me or what I felt to be true? It appeared that life was telling me that God was a liar. At least that is how I was starting to interpret it.

That is when I decided to ask God for His perspective. Here is what I felt Him saying to me:

> *"Your whole life is defined by Me. Circumstances of life seem random and without knowing why they occur they bring doubt, discouragement, despair – death. Look to Me and have Me define and explain the realities of what is really going on. On earth things appear to be dying. You might go through tough situations and become depressed. Take heart! I am with you. I am taking you through the events of your life to grow you, teach you, bless you, and reward you. The things that seem to be the straw that broke the camel's back is really the sand that tips the scales in your favor. Your faith is strengthened. Your love is unconditional. And, your ministry is effective. I am your hope. Without Me there is nothing. Heaven is eternity with Me. Eternity with perfect love, understanding, and joy. Now your awareness is dimmed. It will improve. In heaven, it will be perfected. It will be worth it. Devote your life for the things in heaven."*

Notice He did not change the circumstances. What He did was to refine how I was interpreting what was going on. This little exchange with my Heavenly Father opened me to receive new direction. A few days later I was able to receive instruction from Him to let me know I was pushing at a door that He was closing. He was in fact leading me down a different path and the failure I was feeling was really how I was interpreting His redirection in my life.

Truth is whatever God says is true. We all have events in our lives that we have interpreted incorrectly that are creating a false worldview which we are living out of. We have to let go of our understanding and feelings of these events and have God define them. As long as there is pain when you think about some event in your life, there is still a need of God's redefinition. God is always in control. He is for you. He loves you. And, He can work through every circumstance for the good of those who love Him. He redeems. He restores. He is for you. Take heart. He will never leave you alone. He looks on you with love. Bask in His love for you right now and give Him thanks for His hand on your life.

Step 4: We Have an Enemy that Uses Our False Beliefs Against Us

Most of Christianity falls into one of two fallacies when it comes to our enemy: 1. everything evil is their fault or 2. there is not practical reason to address them. The former gives them too much power; the later gives them too little. They are a defeated foe, but they still cause havoc in believers' lives.

One of the major themes so far has been how we believe lies. Satan is the father of lies, so we have to believe that the demonic is helping either feed us lies or helping us maintain them. Just as it is important to believe that God uses all things to bring us into intimacy, the demonic also uses all they can to place lies into our heart to separate us from God. Remember we are at war and the goal of this battle is the things that would affect God the most: the hearts of you and me.

It is so important to understand that God, at the core of His being, is in love with you. Nothing gives Him more pleasure than you spending time with Him. At the same time, nothing saddens Him more than seeing you separated from Him.

Our enemy hates God, and we are the only things they can reach to get back at God. This is why we are the heart of each battle. Whenever you choose to believe God over what you are experiencing, the demonic gets angrier. They hate God. They hate you.

Just as God looks for every open door of faith to bless you, the demonic look for every open door of sin to feed you lies. The demonic are tricky enemies, but they are also predictable. They will look for every opportunity to influence you from becoming the person God created you to be. Every open door will be a mouthpiece for the demonic to tell you why you cannot live out who you were created to be. Even a slight detour from your destiny is enough of a victory for them to attack with all their might.

The demonic are legalistic. They will not leave until you close the door AND tell them to go. And even then they will wait to make sure you are confident in your position. Josh McDowell used to describe our outlook toward spiritual warfare as a policeman directing traffic. The policeman can easily be run over by a car, but because they know the authority that has been given to them they can stand in the middle of the street and know they will not get hurt. The cars stop and go at their direction because of the badge on their chest. Authority has been given to them, and the drivers have to obey them.

Spiritual warfare is the same. If you do not enforce the rules, the demonic will continue to feed you lies even after you have closed the doors. You have to step up and tell them to leave. Not because you are stronger or braver, but because Jesus has defeated them and given you authority.

Do not be surprised if the demonic tries to spook you when you try to step into your role of authority. They are just testing you. They don't want you to step into your authority, so they see if they can discourage you. Just remember whatever power that the enemy can demonstrate, God is more powerful. It is not even a fair competition. God is vastly superior.

You should not get caught up in this step, but you should be aware of its need. Tell them, "In Jesus name, I command you to go to the foot of the cross. Leave now." You may have to say this more than once. They will test you. But hold firm. If you feel they are not leaving. Ask God to show you if there is another foothold you have not addressed. Make your focus be on God and not them.

This is the reason this is the last step. Ideally, by the time you get to this point, you have closed all the doors, and the demonic just fall off. Again, let me remind you not to do any of these steps alone. One of the demonic's goals is to isolate you from the body. They know that the Christian is vulnerable in isolation. It's the same strategy used in the wild by the predatory cats. They have to separate their prey from the herd in order to overcome it. The herd provides protection, but alone the victim is easy prey.

The Wicked Witch of the West

The demonic is a defeated enemy, but they are counting on you not knowing this. In the book version of The Wizard of Oz, Dorothy was taken to the Wicked Witch of the West by the flying monkeys. When the witch saw what Dorothy had in the gifts from the Good Witch, she became very afraid to the point wanting to run. But then she saw into Dorothy's eyes and could tell that she did not know what she had. The witch knew that she could still make Dorothy her slave because Dorothy did not know how to use the power she had been given. The only thing the witch could do was to deceive Dorothy in thinking she did not have the power that had been given to her. The demonic uses this same strategy.

Do not let the demonic have a mouthpiece into your life. Close all doors, then tell them to leave. Just as you don't want them to be your focus, you also shouldn't ignore them. Know your rights and get them out.

The goal of these four steps (Generational Sins, Wrong Beliefs, Misinterpreted Past, and Evil Spirits) is to repair the root causes and pressures of the addiction. Once these repairs have been made, then the normal maintenance steps are more possible. One major key to walking through these steps is being able to hear the voice of God. This is the next chapter.

6

HEARING GOD'S VOICE

The Voice of the Enemy

I have heard said that the biggest problem in the church today is that it does know how to differentiate the voice of God and the voice of enemy. I would like to argue that this statement is correct.

I can understand how others may cringe at this thought. We know that satan is our accuser. He is looking to steal from you, kill your desire, and destroy your life. He hates you. How can the church possibly mistake that terrible voice with the loving Father?

Easy, we think voice of the enemy is our own voice. Have you ever had thoughts of shame, depression, and unworthiness? Where do they originate? Do you really hate yourself? Does God hate you? No, the demonic hates you. They are the ones who want to see you fail and want to keep you from walking into all that God has for you.

It is incredibly important to know that not every thought in our heads is our own. The reason the demonic is so effective is that they speak to us in ways that sounds like our own thoughts. We are driving along the interstate and have a thought to run off the road. We don't do it, but we are shocked we just had the thought. Where did that come from?

It is the demonic's equivalent to a Hail Mary pass. They are just trying to sneak something by you to end your life. The enemy comes to steal, kill, and destroy (John 10:10). The evil behind this approach is not as much that they are trying to get you to commit suicide, but then they blame you for the thought. You start questioning yourself. You are afraid to tell anyone of your thoughts for fear that they think you're crazy. So you start to live in fear you may just do it someday.

The demonic not only sends you these long shot messages; they also feed you daily lies to keep you from believing God. As a believer, you have the Spirit of God living in you guiding you in all truth. God created you to have intimacy with Him, so in your deepest being you desire to be in agreement with God. Finally, we know that the enemy is the father of lies. Therefore whenever we think lies, we know their source is ultimately not from us.

The Voice of God

The clue to the voice of God is also found in John 10:10. "But I have come that you may have life and life more abundantly." God's words bring life (John 6:68).

It is important to know the source of what we are listening. One will lead us to life; the other will lead us to death. Success in our Christian walk is dependent on this awareness. If freedom is found in having correct beliefs about God and self and if correct beliefs are given by God, then knowing the voice of God is essential.

This first step to hearing from God is to believe that He still speaks. Jesus tells the Pharisees that they didn't hear God's voice because they didn't belong to God. He also said that anyone who does belong to God hears what God says (John 8:46). As believers we have this right and responsibility to hear from God. If He desires intimacy than we must expect that He wants to speak to us.

Henry Blackaby laid out four different ways to hear our Heavenly Father in Experiencing God. He said that God speaks through the Bible, prayer, circumstances, and the Church. While I agree these are the primary ways God speaks, I will add one more:

everything. This is really covered in Blackaby's definition of circumstances, but I believe we need to highlight God's heart here. When we are looking to God, He can and will use all things to speak to us. He loves us and wants to always be in relation to us.

For example, my wife and I were once up in upstate New York checking out a waterfall. We were walking along the trail to the falls when a man and his dog came up. The dog was playful and jumped up on us. We were fine with it as we love dogs and we were outside. But the man apologized and said that the dog was always embarrassing him. Immediately I felt a pain at those words. So when we parted, I told my wife what I was feeling. We prayed about it, and God reminded me of a time when my mom was on the phone with someone. I had done something, and she told the person on the other line that it was just Kevin; he is always embarrassing me. God showed me I had taken that lie to heart as an identity statement about myself that I was an embarrassment. We took this to the Lord to break the lie and find God's truth. He told me how much He was proud of me and how He like to show me off to His friends.

For another example, I was driving one morning to the gym. I was trying to refocus on Jesus instead of random stresses of the day and the period of personal transition I was going through. As I drove over a local river, all of sudden a bald eagle took flight and flew over me. I have only seen bald eagles in the wild maybe twice, and each time they were so far away that I had talked myself into believing that was what they really were. This time he was probably 10 yards from me at most. He was so close that my 2 year old in the back seat kept repeating his mouth was orange.

Obviously a sight like this sticks with you. But, I realized there was something more to this and asked God. I believed He said that this eagle represented me and that I was beginning to take flight and soar. This experience of the bald eagle has since brought encouragement and motivation during that transition period.

The point of these two examples is to keep attentive to when God may be speaking to you. You don't need to make a spiritual connection to everything you do, but if you are open to having God making connections to your circumstances, you may find the answers you need to get you where He is taking you.

The Difference Between the Two

How do we differentiate between the voice of the enemy and the voice of God? The more we know the character of God; the more we will know His voice. He loves us; He believes in us; and He will lead us to hope and life. (If you doubt any of this read Romans 8 multiple times.)

This is so important because you will live out of the voice you are listening to. If you believe the lies the devil throws at you that you are worthless, a failure, and that those you love would be better off without you, then you will not live out of the unique calling God placed into your life. Instead you will try to be whomever you can that would cause you the least amount of pain. If you believe that if people knew the real you they would reject you, then you will always live your life behind a mask so nobody would ever know the real you.

So how do you know to which voice you are listening? Look at the fruit. If the thoughts are leading you into life, peace and freedom, it is from Holy Spirit. If it leads to depression, pain, fear, and immobility, then it is from the enemy.

When we understand that God loves us, then we will know that He will never belittle us, discourage us, or put us down. That is the voice of the enemy. God will always offer us hope and make us feel like we can accomplish anything. Because, of course, that is what He promised in Scripture. "We can do all things through Christ who strengthens us" (Philippians 4:13).

Shame vs. Conviction

Even conviction can come in either form. True conviction comes not at the sound of God's displeasure in us, but at the moment He turns the light on brightly enough for us to see our imperfections. His light does not expose us to His anger. But, in love He wants us to correct the errors keeping us from more of Him. He exposes painful issues in our hearts, so we can bring them to Him for healing. Without the conviction of Holy Spirit, we do not change and grow. Satan is the one that points out sin to shame us and create fear that will lead us away from God and others.

Shame tells us we need to measure up in order to be accepted. However, none of us are perfect. We all have our faults, so we struggle with performing to others' expectations. Therefore, when we hear instruction to turn from sin, we sense displeasure about who we are, thinking it is just another reminder that we will never measure up.

John 3 tells us He did not come into the world to condemn it but to save it. God loves us. What we don't understand is that God loves us more than we want Him to. When He sees error in our lives that is hindering us from experiencing all He has for us, He lovingly wants to remove the issue, so that we would no longer be defined by it but defined by God.

It is important to discern the voice of who is speaking to us. The voice of God, even when exposing sin, offers hope and life. The voice of the demonic comes to steal, kill and destroy. Even though the voice of the enemy may point out facts, it will create fear and lead you away from God. God never uses shame to motivate us toward right living or excellence. He never motivates us by withholding His love from us.

The Word of God is Living and Active

For the word of God is living and active. Sharper than any double-edged sword, it penetrates even to dividing soul and spirit, joints and marrow; it judges the thoughts and attitudes of the heart. – Hebrews 4:12

This is a wonderful verse that solidifies the importance of the Scripture. Coupled with 2 Timothy 3:16, the Bible is the very breath of God that goes to the inmost being of people to accomplish its purposes. Scripture is what our Lord shot back at satan in the wilderness, and it is the one offensive weapon described in the full armor of God. The Bible is essential to our staying close to God and maintaining right thinking.

But in regards to this Hebrews passage, we typically limit the message of this verse by only thinking of the Bible. This is not what the author of Hebrews had in mind.

The first four chapters of Hebrews describe how God spoke in the past, how the Israelites heard His voice, and how we are to pay attention to what we have heard. Three times leading to the verse in 4:12, the author quotes Psalm 95:7-8: "Today, if you hear His voice, do not harden your hearts." The connotation of this passage is that the word of God is the voice of the Spirit communicating to you. It most definitely can be applied to the Bible, but it also means so much more.

When we come to God in our pain, we need to take time to listen to what the Spirit is saying to us. This verse tells us the word of God judges the thoughts and attitudes of the heart. Listening to what the Spirit has to say illuminates the lies in our hearts that are keeping us from fully believing the truths of God. The Spirit, who searches our hearts, can reword these truths in ways that speak right into the pain in our lives for us to receive its truth.

My cousin once lost her three month old son to sudden infant death syndrome (SIDS). As a parent myself, I felt the pain and sorrow that her family was going through. In the midst of this pain, it is difficult to read the passages of God's love, God's plan, God's goodness and have faith to believe it is true for them. The family was left with two options: 1. to kill the desire to know why or 2. to have an encounter with God that changes them. Choosing the first option deadens Christianity; choosing the second lives out Hebrews 4:12.

God's word in this context is God speaking to reword His truth in ways that penetrate them past our pain and experience so we can hear and believe them. In His love for us God enters into our pain in order that our relationship may be renewed.

I do not know exactly the words my cousin needed to hear from God at that time, nor am I saying this would have been an easy step. What I am saying is that the voice of our Father is kind and gentle. He does not break the bruised reed (Matthew 12:20). He goes after the lost sheep (Matthew 18:14). He never leaves nor forsakes us (Hebrews 13:5). All of this is true because He loves us beyond what we can ever imagine possible. And, in His love He will come to us and meet us in our time of need. As we draw near to Him, He will draw near to us (James 4:8).

What If I Hear God Wrong?

Have you ever considered the implications of God asking Abraham to sacrifice Isaac? Sure everything ends up wonderful and Isaac is spared. Sure it is a profound analogy of God offering up Jesus. But, have you ever considered that God asked Abraham to do something God did not want him to do?

God told Abraham to offer up his son as a sacrifice. Then God stops Abraham before he could follow through with it. Did God change His mind?

The thing that gets me is that God seems to lead us into situations and even leads us into decisions through prayer that He does not want us to ultimately follow through on. He seems to be getting us to a point of obedience that we would go and do whatever and then because of our willingness to do that first thing, He leads us into something even better. This is what happened to Abraham.

This is also what happened to David. He is chased all over Israel by Saul. Then on two separate occasions God gives Saul into David's hands. Both times David could have easily ended all of his running around and moved forward with the word he was given about being king, but both times he feels that God does not want him to harm Saul.

I don't claim to understand all of God's ways, and I hope you don't either. What I do know is that He is intentional with us. He is leading us down a path where we will have greater freedom from sin, greater power over the enemy, and greater joy in our lives. He is a loving Father that wants His best for His children.

I feel God has acted this way with my family as we have tried to adopt. My wife and I felt very clearly that we were to try to adopt an Asian orphan. We went through the home studies, applications, and thousands of dollars to get our application in country. We were months away from a referral when we were postponed by the announcement that we were pregnant with our second child.

Two years later we felt the strong urge again to try to adopt. Because of the time that passed, we had to redo the home studies, paperwork and thousands of dollars. This time we got a referral of a little girl that was 3 days older than our youngest girl. Two weeks after getting the referral, the referring country removed her from us saying she was accidently promised to another family.

Both times we have felt very clearly that we were to start the adoption process. Both times we have given a lot of our time and money into trying to be obedient. We may have mis-heard His direction. We may also have heard Him correctly, but He did not want us to finish the adoption. Maybe the answer is another unknown alternative. I don't know the answer to that yet. I do know that God loves and rewards faith and obedience (John 14:15 and Hebrews 11:6).

It is several years removed from that second attempt. We have since moved to this country to work with orphan girls. As of yet we have never been able to adopt, but we have no doubt that God used those two attempts to get us to where we are now.

Most people are fearful of listening to God because they are afraid of putting words in God's mouth. They are afraid they will move forward on something only to find out God was not in it. If we are ever to be successful in the Christian walk, we need to get over this fear. Christianity is based on a relationship with God, and relationships are built on communication. We need to listen to His voice and obey what He says.

The point is not to be as concerned with getting it wrong as it is about not obeying what you have heard. A guaranteed recipe to get the silence of God is to not obey what God has told you. I'm not against you getting wise counsel, but I don't think wise counsel would have agreed with Abraham regarding Isaac. Wise counsel was not leading Jesus to the cross. Cover everything you do with love and be open to God's redirection, and you will be fine. I don't believe that God will question us about what we believed He told us when we get to heaven. I do believe He will hold us accountable to our obedience of what we heard.

Take time to listen to what God is saying to you. He is not quiet. He calls each of His own by name. His followers listen and recognize His voice (John 10:3-4). God's love for you is the motivation for all His communication with you. His words lead to life because they are life. His intentions for you are good. Go to Him. Listen to His voice. He is calling you to peace and rest.

We are to grow in hearing and understanding His voice. It is for our benefit and protection. It will be a foundational tool to finding freedom. Ignoring the voice of God renders us helpless in battling out of addiction.

7

CORRECTING THE LIES

"We demolish arguments and every pretension that sets itself up against the knowledge of God, and we take captive every thought to make it obedient to Christ."
– 2 Corinthians 10: 5

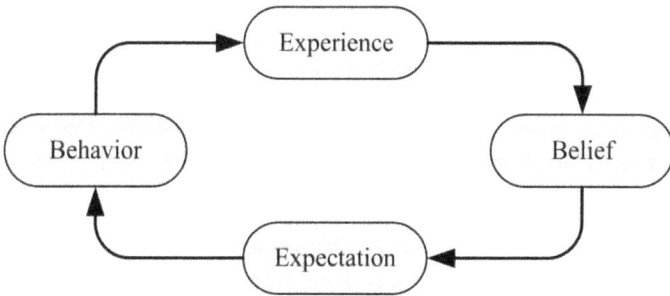

Breaking the Cycle

We need to be able to hear God's voice if we are to break the cycle. Whatever God says is true; the experiences and circumstances of life are just facts. They really happened, but our minds will always try to synthesize that message so we can understand it. Therefore we form beliefs based on our understanding of the facts, and those beliefs form the expectations we hold about life. Since we believe that is the way life works, we set expectations in accordance to those beliefs. In order to create harmony in our lives, our behaviors follow these experiences that support the beliefs we hold. Therefore this entire cycle is run on the beliefs we hold, and where those beliefs are wrong, the cycle takes us away from God's best.

As a Christian, all sin is based out of a lie that we are believing, and most of the times, it is based out multiple lies. These lies we believe reside in our unconscious reasoning and formed over many years of interpreting our life events. If these lies where ever exposed to our conscious minds, we would more than likely agree they are lies. The issue is not whether we intellectually agree to the lies; it is whether or not they feel true. What we feel is true is what we live out of.

Two particular lies that I felt to be true and built into my addiction with pornography were: "no one will love me" and "I do not deserve love, so I will need to take it from others." These lies led to an expectation that I would not experience love from others. Therefore my behavior became doing things to gain feelings of being loved. This type of self-gratification tends to turn people off thus "proving" in my mind that no one will love me. I have thereby created a self-fulfilling cycle. All of this started from my interpretations of my experiences and the adherence to false beliefs.

The story of the prodigal son is a good example of how false beliefs lead to destructive actions (Luke 15:11-31). Near the end of the parable the older son explains to the father why he is not coming in to join the party. He basically shares his view that his father treats him as a slave. He works hard every day for his father's recognition and is never appreciated. He viewed his father as a cruel taskmaster, and now that his younger rebellious brother has come back from his partying, he is the one that gets celebrated by their father. Why go to a party that would remind him of his pain?

You can interpret that the younger son did not feel the love of the father either. That is why he left. "I'm working like a slave. I would be better off without my father lording over me." Even when he decides to come back, it is based on knowing his father had lots of slaves. Neither son knew the love their father had for them.

What was the truth of the father's love? The father loved both of his sons. He wanted the older son to come into the party. He reminded him that everything he owned was his. The younger son was also shown love from the father by reinstating him as a son even after the pain and embarrassment he caused his father.

The lies the sons believed made them think they either must do something in order to be blessed by their father or that they could not do enough so they might as well give up. Even in our age of grace, many people think the same thoughts about God. The truth of the new covenant is that nothing can keep me from the blessing of God except the deception that I must either do something in order to receive it or the deception that I must kill the desire to be blessed because I will never receive it.

It is important to believe in truth. An incorrect view of life, God, or self will lead to harmful choices and decisions. These choices and decisions will strengthen the lies and will move us even further from God. That is why we not only need to believe truth, but also to root out the lies.

Common Lies Christians Believe

For example, let's say you view yourself as a sinner. This is a common one among Christians because they mistakenly think it is how God still views them. God sees you as a saint. You were a sinner. For those who have asked Christ into your life, you are now hid in Christ.

If you do happen to see yourself as a sinner, you may set an expectation that at some point you are going to fail. Therefore in your behaviors you tend to not commit all the way because you assume you will soon sin. Since you do not commit fully, you do fail and you say to yourself, "See, I am a sinner."

Calling yourself a sinner, a worm, nobody special is not being humble. When you are humble, you only call yourself those things God says about you– nothing more and nothing less. God calls you His sons and daughters. You are His friends. You are a royal priesthood. He no longer sees anything negative in you. If you want to live up to His plan for your life, you will need to see yourself as He sees you.

Let's also consider the lie that all temptation is a sin. This one is extremely dangerous for those struggling with addiction. First of all, we need to realize this is a lie, and the best way to point it out would be to understand that Jesus was tempted in every way just as us yet was without sin (Hebrews 4:15). Temptations cannot be sin, therefore, there must be some point where we can deal with the temptation and still remain pure.

The problem is we give in too easily when we believe the lie about temptation being sin. We get tempted, feel like we have already sinned, and then give in to what we were tempted to do because we already feel that we failed. Those times we don't give in to the temptations, we still beat ourselves up for even considering the evil we were tempted to do. We feel so guilty about the temptation that we don't tell anyone and fall into isolation.

We have to realize that demons whisper temptations to us. Actions start with thoughts; outward sins start in the inward mind (James 1:13-15). How we deal with these whispers determine our success.

The demonic knows your weaknesses. They have spent your lifetime forming them in you. They know the whispers that trigger you to believe lies that lead to unholy action. These whispers may give clues to the lies we believe, but they don't determine the men and women we are. We are saints, and dealing with these temptations refines our saintliness; it doesn't diminish it.

Remember the demonic is not like God. While they can put thoughts into our heads, they cannot read our thoughts. If you want to deal with the demonic, you have to tell them to go. Trying to ignore the temptations by thinking on something else leaves them hanging around to whisper the lies again. Realizing they are not coming from you helps you to tell them to leave and to get help to tell them to leave. Don't let a thief hang around your house because they will only rob you once your defenses are down.

Making Agreements with Our Lies

Sometimes our lies lay under the surface of our thinking; other times we have come into full-fledged agreements with them. These agreements or vows hold stronger weight because of the verbal affirmation of the lies about how we will react or behave. Instead of hiding in our subconscious subtly affecting our behaviors, these vows affect our behaviors more quickly and have created walls of beliefs to maintain them. Because of the outward agreement, these are harder to view as lies and will take more time to dismantle.

Let's take the example of seeing yourself as a sinner. If you believe this lie, then you will assume your natural tendency is to sin and you will always fail. After awhile you will get fed up with the cycle of sin, confess, sin, confess, sin, etc., and most Christians make one of two different vows.

1. I will never tell anyone of my struggles. Your embarrassment pushes you to hide from what you believe to be true about yourself – you are a sinner, messed up to the core.

2. I will never do that sin again. You get fed up with the cycle, so you will commit to freedom on your own strength.

The first leads to isolation and depression. The second leads to a Pharisaical lifestyle and separation from God. Neither leads to the freedom offered in the Scriptures.

In general, vows are our own attempts to protect ourselves from the agonizing pain of the lies we believe. They are promises we make to ourselves, which are designed to distance us from the pain. What they really accomplish is to distance us from God. God often takes us to the pain in our lives to reveal the lies, but our vows keep us from going there with Him and thus we never properly deal with the lies that are causing all of the pain.

The devil loves to help us keep the vows in place. If our vows are ever successful in keeping the pain at bay, the voice of the enemy reinforces the need to keep the vow. If the vow is ever not successful, the enemy shames us by making us feel that we need to try harder at keeping the vow.

Here are some examples of possible vows:

1. I will never trust God (him) again. I will never talk to God (him) again. I will never listen to God (him) again. I will never be vulnerable again.

2. I will be invisible (go away). I will make them love me (by becoming the boy Daddy always wanted; by trying really hard; by being perfect; by never making a mistake, etc.) I will never let anyone close enough to hurt me like that ever

again. I will be very good. I will make myself into an acceptable person. I give up.

3. I will never trust anybody again. I will take care of them. I will be better than them. I will show them. I will do it alone. I will do it myself.

4. I will hurry up and die. I will not be here. I will not give of myself. I give up. I'll never try.

Peter's Vow to Jesus

Even vows that seem good are not. Think of Peter's vow to Jesus about laying down his life for Jesus (John 13:37). We would think this is a noble statement, but Jesus knew that Peter's idea was not the same as the life he had for Peter. Peter made the statement out of a belief that the way of the kingdom was direct confrontation; after all didn't Jesus tell them to get swords (Luke 22:36-28). Jesus had something else in mind altogether.

While Peter was thinking about the overthrow of the Roman occupation, Jesus saw Peter's denial of Him. Peter's vow was to lay down his life for Jesus (John 13:38), and in the garden Peter tries this by grabbing a sword and attacking the soldiers. Jesus not only stops him, but also heals the ear Peter just cut off. Jesus then gives Himself over to the soldiers (John 18:10-12).

Peter was willing to go it alone against the mob, and he would have very likely died. How dare Jesus stop Peter from fulfilling his vow? In his kindness Jesus stopped him from making a foolish mistake and missing God's best.

Even in the midst of God's grace, all Peter could see was that Jesus stopped his wholehearted devotion. This sends confusion into the camp of Jesus' friends, and they scatter. Peter and John decide to follow Jesus into the high priest's courtyard. Then, just as Jesus predicted, Peter denies Jesus three times.

How can someone who vowed to die for Jesus so suddenly deny him? Peter had created a vow that God did not allow for him to fulfill. Becoming disillusioned Peter did not have courage to muster up anymore.

Did God thwart Peter's vow? No. Peter thwarted Peter's vow because he made a vow from a basis of a lie that it was all about him. Your vows actually keep you from God because they keep your focus on the wrong thing – yourself and not God.

We always hear about Peter being reinstated by the three-fold affirmation of his love. But one thing that Jesus did that is often overlooked is that Jesus purified His vow. Jesus said, yes you will die for me. But this is the way you will do it. The way you were planning on doing it would bring you glory. What I'm calling you to will bring Me glory (John 21:18-19).

How Do I Stop Sinning Without Making Commitments to Stop?

If Peter's vow was bad, certainly our vows to abstain from our addictions are bad. I know this sounds blasphemous. How do we stop without making commitments to stop?

We must understand God is not as concerned about our sins as we are. When we put our trust in God all of our sins were forgiven – past, present and future. Now, our sin points us to something greater.

Let me state that I don't think your sins are unimportant. Sin is still bad, and it still hurts those around you. There are consequences to sin. However, God is no longer affected by your sin. All of His hatred for it went to the Cross. He can now work on your healing.

Sin lets us know there are areas in our hearts that need healing. When we are so focused on stopping the sin, we neglect dealing with our hearts. When we sin, we need to ask God what are the lies or vows we are believing that is leading to this sin. Confessing and breaking these vows will lead to the freedom you seek. Once these are dealt with, right behavior becomes so much easier.

Breaking the Lies and Vows

We deal with the lies and vows the same way; we need to confess them, thank God for His forgiveness, reject our agreements to them, and then receive the truth God wants us to take on. This is how "we demolish arguments and every pretension that sets itself up against the knowledge of God, and take captive every thought to make it obedient to Christ" (2 Corinthians 10:5). And, we must actively take captive every thought because the enemy lies to us. He is the father of lies. If we believe his lies, we will reject God's truth. His lies will always lead us away from God (John 8:43-45).

The truth is what sets us free. But, we must hold to the teachings. We must actively work at believing the truth over the lies (John 8:31-32). Holding on to Jesus' teaching is walking out the truth. This is how we start to experience His truth as real and find freedom. Here are some simple steps to help you break the lies and vows:

Step 1: Write Down the Lie.

This is important as it keeps you focused instead of allowing you to drift off in abstracts. It also allows you to pinpoint the lie as it affects you. The more specific you can be will help you to more powerfully attack the lie with which you are struggling. A common place for lies to reside is in how you view yourself – identity statements. These statements often start, "I am a…" or "I always/never…"

Step 2: Confess the Lie.

Believe the lie is sin, and deal with it as sin. Confess it. Confess your sin of believing the lie of… stating it exactly as you wrote it down.

Step 3: Thank God for Your Forgiveness.

Thanksgiving is oil that greases the Spirit's movement in your life. You have been given the free gift of grace and forgiveness. Thankfulness should be our first response. "I thank You for Your forgiveness." You will find the Christian life easier if you practice the discipline of thanksgiving.

Step 4: Offer Forgiveness.

You probably have had people who contributed to helping you form the lie. Forgive them freely as you have been forgiven. Forgiveness is extremely important to God and withholding forgiveness will stunt your freedom. You will also need to forgive yourself and God. Remember forgiveness is not so much for the other person or for God; it is for you. You are choosing to release the other person from the pain you feel they caused you.

Step 5: Actively Turn from the Lie.

Many Christians fuse confession and repentance. They are closely linked but still need to be separate steps in the process. Confession says you agree with God that believing the lie was a sin. Repentance actively renounces your agreements to the lie and to satan. "I renounce my agreement to the lie: ... I break off any effects from belief in this lie."

Step 6: Receive God's Truth.

You cannot just turn from a lie; you have to turn to the truth (2 Timothy 2:22). This is why the previous chapter is so important. Once you have cleared your connection with the lie, you are now free to hear what God says is true. Listen to what Holy Spirit tells you. Ask God to show you His truth that powerfully attacks the lies.

For example, I had a lie I believed: "I am not worthy to receive anything good from God." The truth is to specifically address the lie. Ephesians 1:3 tells me that God has blessed me in the heavenly realms with every spiritual blessing. That is true, but it does not fully attack the lie I was believing. The voice of God on the other hand is sharper than any two edge sword (Hebrews 4:12). What I felt that God told me was, "I am worthy because God said I am worthy; therefore, there is no good thing that God would withhold from me." Now that is a truth that can set me free.

What Are the Lies We Believe?

Here is a short list of lies which you could be believing. It is not complete, but it can jump-start your brainstorming on what may be keeping you down. Take note of those that feel true to you. You may intellectually not agree with a statement, but if it feels true, then you may be living your life as if it is true.

- No one will love me for who I am.
- I must isolate myself from others so I don't get hurt again.
- I am not worthy to receive anything good from God.
- If people knew the real me they would reject me.

- I have messed up so badly I have missed God's best for me.
- My value comes from what I do, not from who I am.
- Even when I give my best, it is not good enough.
- If I take time off to relax, God will be upset.
- The world is more fun than God.
- I must keep my thoughts and feelings to myself because they are not important.
- Authority figures cannot be trusted to care for me.
- I am not competent as a man/woman.
- I will always be a failure.
- My wife/husband/kids would be better off without me.
- God loves others more than me.
- I will always be on the outside looking in.
- I cannot trust God or feel secure with Him, because He has let me down.
- It is a mark of failure to be tempted.
- God would not choose to speak to me.
- I blend into the crowd; I am nobody special.
- I cannot receive complements.
- Things never work out for me.
- Someone else could do a better job than me.

Ask God to show you if there are any other lies that feel true to you.

Each one of these statements is a lie. You need to confess and repent so that you can receive God's truth. God created you. He does not create failures. To live out of any of these lies is to not live the life you were created for.

To be candid, each one of the lies listed above is a lie that I have believed. Is it any wonder that I could not fully give myself over to God? I needed God to reinterpret the grid in which I was living. I needed to receive more of His love before I would ever be willing to love Him more – much less anyone else.

Putting It Into Practice

Going through these steps breaks the legal power to the lies, but you will need to choose to keep the doors shut. If a lie ventures back into your brain, reject it immediately in the name of Jesus and confess your belief in the truth God has given you. It will take time for the truth to take root as you have had your entire life thinking those lies were true. You have established behavior and judgments based on the lies. It will take repetition and prayer to start living out of the truth. But take heart, it will get easier; it is the way you were created to live.

Pray through your truths daily to reprogram your mind until they feel true. Do this at least for 30 days, but you may decide to do it longer for those lies that felt more true. Once you feel you can move from these daily reminders, it is important to still keep them nearby for the seasons when those lies try to take root again.

Take each of the truths God has given you and find Bible verses that support those thoughts. Doing this helps you meditate on the truth and give confirmation that what God has shown you is true. Use a concordance or an on-line Bible tool to help you with your search. Many times you will find verses that you had previously ignored or explained away because of the lies you had believed.

Another tool to reprogram your thinking is worship songs. Singing allows truth to seep deep into your heart. It rehearses

God's truth and allows its power to transcend your intellectual beliefs. This is why music is so important. You may listen to secular music passing it off saying you like the beat, but you are feeding your soul with the world's system and values. I'm not encouraging legalistic hatred for secular music, but what you feed yourself will form who you are (Galatians 6:7-8).

Find songs that relate to the truths God gave to you or find one that seems to affect you. Play it over and over. Sing it. While worship is warfare against our enemy, it also strengthens you by reminding you how God sees you and the world. Those that regularly practice worshipping will find their freedom.

Sometimes exposing the lies does not take the power away from them. Sometimes you need to disarm the hook where the lies entered your life. This is what we will go over next: allowing Jesus to reinterpret past events.

8

ALLOWING JESUS TO REINTERPRET PAST EVENTS

Why Wrong Beliefs Feel True

All of the lies that feel true are based off of our interpretations of life events. These interpretations give weight to what we believe. Sometimes confessing the lies just isn't enough; sometimes we need to invite God to reinterpret the life events behind the lie.

I Was Too Young To Interpret Life On My Own

God says that He works through all things for the good of those who love Him, but often we hold onto experiences that we say that God let us down. These experiences can be very traumatic, such as molestation, violence, emotional abuse, etc. or they can be painful interpretations of events.

For me one to the painful events was highlighted with my family's annual trip to the fair. Alongside the excitement of the rides and food, I always carried a fear of getting lost or abandoned at the fair. This fear was realized every year with getting separated from my family at least once. Knowing this was a common experience we had a pre-arranged spot to get back together. Every year I would sit balled up on the wall in front of the First Aid Center waiting for my parents to come get me. There was a couple times as an elementary school kid where I waited so long that I left the fair to go find the car to make sure they hadn't gone home without me. Each time my parents came to get me, I was told again to make sure to keep close and not wander off.

I came away feeling it was my fault. I was careless. I needed to be more responsible. These were traumatic experiences for me, which fed several other lies into my thoughts:

I am nobody special; I blend into the crowd. My parents would be better off without me. I would eventually be abandoned by those I loved. Nobody would care for me, because I was too much of a burden. I'm a failure.

This is not an exercise to blame my parents. I actually had very good parents. They did their best to love me and care for me. If this would happen to either of my girls, I would be very scared and would have the tendency to exhort them similarly. The point is I was too young to interpret these traumatic events on my own, and the demonic was all too eager to help me out.

These experiences played a vital role in forming a deep fear in my life of eventually being abandoned. I finally came to a point of exposing the lies of abandonment and allowing God to show me truth. While I was experiencing growth, these abandonment feelings were still strong. It wasn't until I was praying with leader in my church about them that God brought up the experiences from the fair. As I shared this, he told me it wasn't my fault. It is the role of the parent to watch over and protect their kids.

It was like his words lifted a weight off of me. I needed this older, wiser man to speak into my situation and reinterpret it as God saw it. This realization took the sting out of those memories for me. It also released the pressure that I had to work to keep people from abandoning me.

How Misinterpreted Events Form Our View of God

Jack and Julie are good friends of my wife and me. Shortly after they were married, Julie started having physical issues that installed fear into both of them. Since we were nearby at the time, we had the opportunity to pray with them.

During one point of prayer, I felt an impression to ask Jack about abandonment. He was unsure but was open to pray and ask God about it. As we did he remembered that as a young kid being dropped off at a boarding school. He remembered feeling fear and confusion as he saw his parents driving away. He would get so homesick he would throw up. He felt abandoned by his parents at a time he really needed them.

As with so many people, Jack subconsciously interpreted God being the same way. If God is his Heavenly Father, then He must be like his dad. Jack felt God would be absent any time he needed His help.

Now newly married, his young wife started having scary physical issues, and Jack finds himself in a dilemma. He really needs God's help, but he has an underlying belief that God is not going to be there. This belief handcuffs his prayers, and Jack once again feels like the helpless kid watching his parents drive off without him.

As we continued to pray with Jack, we ask Jesus to show Jack where He was during this time. Jack mentally saw Jesus standing right beside him holding his hand. All of a sudden the pain of that situation subsides as Jack realizes he wasn't alone. He was now able to receive the truth that God is our ever-present help in time of need (Psalm 46:1).

There were other things that this memory brought up, but for the moment this was the thing that Jack needed. He previously couldn't engage to help his new wife because it was a painful reminder of his feelings of abandonment. He couldn't go to God because to him God was just as guilty as his parents. Jack needed that event reinterpreted showing Jesus with him so the pain of feeling abandoned would be removed, and he could then give support and comfort to his wife. Notice also if he had not gotten help and continued to pull away, this situation would have reinforced his fears and led to his wife learning not to count on him when she needed help which would have led to Jack feeling abandoned from her too.

Joseph's Interpretation of Events

Our interpretations of our experiences in life result in our beliefs. These beliefs can come from God who alone can give true interpretations, or they can come from our limited mind, sometimes with the aid of the demonic. Our beliefs result into expectations about life which lead to behaviors. These behaviors, flowing out of our beliefs, create new experiences that tend to support those beliefs, whether good or bad.

Circumstances and experiences lead to facts, but God's Word and promises lead to truth. Instead of using our limited understanding to generate the interpretations of our experiences, we need to turn to God to allow for His interpretations. This is how we break the cycle. We need to change how we develop our beliefs.

Think of Joseph, here is a man that had every right to believe the worst in people. Joseph quickly goes from living under the favor of his father to being rejected by his brothers and living as a slave. His bad circumstances became worse in Egypt as he goes from slavery to prison. We must realize that just because we read this account in a few minutes of our time, Joseph's life played out for many years. He had day after day to think on his rejection – to think of how life could have been.

So finally at the end of Genesis, Joseph is second in command of all Egypt and his brothers come to him begging for forgiveness (Genesis 50:18-20). Do Joseph brothers deserve the forgiveness? Does Joseph have the right and power to execute judgment on them? God had elevated him to this position, could he now take his revenge on them? In the natural, we can answer yes to each of these questions. Joseph could have rightly executed his brothers for their sin.

Joseph did not condemn his brothers because he had a different interpretation of the events. God meant it all for good (Genesis 50:20). His interpretation of those events helped him to accurately respond to the opportunities he was given. Think about it… if Joseph had not forgiven his brothers, he would have killed the biological line that Jesus was going to come from. Jesus does not come from Joseph's lineage; it was from Judah. If Joseph had not forgiven Judah, our hope would have ended.

Process of Healing the Past

The roots of addiction often lie in childhood. If we do not go back and correct our interpretations of past events, the only option for stopping the behavior is through our effort. We need to invite Jesus into those moments and have Him heal our hearts. Here are practical steps to lead you through this process:

Word of Exhortation:

As with any of these steps, it is best to go through them with a mature believer. Most of these events will be emotionally charged which will make them difficult to navigate on your own. A mature believer can help you process without the emotional attachment to the pain and hurt involved.

Also the demonic doesn't want you healed. They will try to manipulate the situation. You should take authority over them at the beginning and anytime fear or discouragement sets in. But above all keep your focus on God and continually invite God's presence over the time.

Step 1: Determine the Event to Reprocess.

There is any number of events where you can start, but it is best to ask Holy Spirit to reveal the hurt or issue He wants to heal. He knows what you are ready for and what will lead to the needed healing. As you ask, listen and watch as He tells or shows the event to you. The event may not make sense at first. I find it best to take it by faith. If you ask what He wants to show you, choose to believe that what is revealed is from Him. Remember, He wants you healed more than you do, and He knows what He is doing.

Step 2: Immerse Yourself in the Memory.

Now that you have a memory to focus on, enter into it fully. Tell the person with you what is going on, who is there, how you felt, etc. Listen to Holy Spirit to tell you what He is trying to show you.

Step 3: Tell Jesus What You Are Feeling.

Pour out your feelings to Jesus. Be honest even if you think Christians are not supposed to feel that way. If you are not real with Him, He cannot reveal to you the root of the pain. Hanging on to the pain of the situation by not expressing it hinders the healing you can receive. It is vital to give all of the pain to Jesus for Him to heal you.

Step 4: Offer Forgiveness.

Unforgiveness will block the healing process. This is incredibly important to God. It is unbiblical for a Christian not to forgive, and it is the greatest advantage you can give to the demonic by not offering forgiveness to those who have hurt you.

No matter what degree of shame or hurt you have experienced, you have a chance to let go of judgment, bitterness, and unforgiveness. Healing comes not just from the acknowledgment of the pain, but the forgiveness you choose to give. Forgiving does not mean denying or excusing the pain you suffered, but rather means letting go of its hold on your heart. The issue is never the capacity to forgive, but whether you desire to forgive.

Many of you may be taken to points in your life that you need to forgive someone that drastically hurt you. You may have been raped, molested, abused, humiliated, or demoralized by someone that should have been trustworthy. It is not that Jesus doesn't care what happened, but the unforgiveness will block the healing that is needed for you.

As in before with the lies, it is probable that you need to forgive yourself and God. The more you walk out forgiving others; the more you will walk out your own forgiveness. We are able to forgive because we have been forgiven. Thank God for forgiving you by forgiving others.

Step 5: Ask Jesus to Show You What He Was Doing.

Now that you have offered forgiveness, think back on the memory and ask Jesus where He is. Do you sense where He is? He is there because He says He will never leave you nor forsake you. Ask Him what He was doing? What does He say actually happened? Wait. Allow Him to speak what you need to hear.

Be sure to share what you see and hear with the person with you. I was praying with someone, and when they saw Jesus, they perceived Him coming toward them with a knife. Obviously, this was not Jesus, but a demon disguised as Jesus trying to confuse and stop the process (2 Corinthians 11:14). Again, it is important to go through this process with a mature believer. In this case, we were able to deal with the demonic, find Jesus, and address the pain and fear.

Step 6: Write Down What Jesus Shows You.

Another reason to speak out whatever you see and hear is that the person with you may write it down. These are the things that Jesus knows you need. There will be truth statements in them that you will need to revisit. He may tell you a new way to view yourself. He may reveal lies you have believed. He may just shed light on your past. These are great things for you to go back and review later. Having someone else write these down allows you to focus on what God is showing you and be present to what He is doing.

It is best to refrain from judging the experience while you are going through it. This will cut short the experience and limit you from entering into Holy Spirit's flow. Remember He is reinterpreting past events for you, so it will not make sense at that time. God's ways are above our ways (Isaiah 55:9). You will have time to go back over everything afterwards. Then you can pray through the experience to help bring understanding on what happened.

If He does reveal lies, break your agreements with them as in the last chapter. With every bit of truth He shows you, repeat them daily until you feel they are true.

Paul's Interpretation of His Current Situation

Getting Jesus' interpretations are also important in your current situations. There is an unusual account about Paul's travels to Jerusalem (Acts 21:10-14). A prophet Agabus tells Paul that he will be bound and handed over to the Gentiles. Then with other believers he pleads with Paul not to go to Jerusalem. Paul would not be dissuaded because he had already been compelled by the Spirit to go to Jerusalem (Acts 20:22).

He eventually does get bound and handed over to the Gentiles and shipped to Rome. And because of this we all benefit because a majority of his writings occur during the new found "free time" in prison. Notice the prophet was correct in the future events he saw, yet the application of what he saw differed from Paul's. If Paul heard the words of Agabus and interpreted them out of fear, we would have missed out on much of Paul's theology and teaching.

We also need to have God interpret our situations. The circumstances in our world may look bad or good, but Jesus alone has the right to interpret them. Jesus said He is the truth (John 14:6). Therefore truth is whatever Jesus says is true. If we live out of any other interpretation, it will lead us down the wrong path.

9

REPAIRING THE WALLS

My Chains Are Gone

Much of what we've covered so far has been about laying a foundation for living effectively in the Christian life. Even so, there is still much you can do to help your freedom. These next few steps going forward are where most Christians focus. You may have tried them many times, and by being still stuck in addiction you kept feeling under the pile. Because you honestly tried these steps so often and seemed to fail, this chapter may feel like a noose being reapplied.

This is not the aim. The goal is not to heap back on the burdens of Christianity, but to highlight how the disciplines of the faith can lead to perpetual freedom. When you tried to apply these disciplines before you were carrying around wrong thinking about God and yourself. These steps were burdens because they were efforts to try to obtain God's love and approval. With the hard work of the previous chapters, you have dealt with many of your barriers to God and the resources He has provided.

Previously you were undermining your own efforts because you had wrong motives. If you thought you were trying to earn God's favor by doing these disciplines, you would not lean on His resources to accomplish them. The truth of the matter is that God often allows life to work in a way that makes living the Christian life in our own strength impossible, so that we learn to trust Him with the whole process. He wants to travel the journey with you. He is not the destination; He is the abundant life.

With much of your wrong beliefs dealt with, you are free to obey God because you want to and free to rely on His provisions because you know He is for you. Joy will flow out of this kind of obedience and be the fuel to further obedience. Now when you fail at obedience, you have tools to discover the root of the matter. Instead of beating yourself over the head with accusations of shame and guilt, you can respond from a place of forgiveness and confidently go to your Heavenly Father for advice and guidance.

These disciplines were never God's effort to put us back under the law. They are tools to help you succeed at the plan He has given you. With that in mind, approach all of it as an opportunity to dive into the never-ending love and respect of the One who made you.

Reading the Bible to Spend Time with the One Who Wrote It

When I was introduced to Jesus, the man preaching encouraged us to not only read the Bible but spend time with the One who wrote it. This is foundational to how we should approach the Bible. The reason it is living and active is because Holy Spirit interacts with it and us to transform our thinking and move it deep into our hearts. When you read it as any other book, your worldview interprets what you are reading before it gets to your conscious mind. With the work you have done breaking lies, you should gain new understanding to what God has always been trying to say to you all along.

Most of Christianity strongly exhorts you to study your Bible. While there is a place for this, oftentimes we apply this by gaining knowledge from the Bible. Again, this sounds good, but Paul warns us that knowledge puffs up (1 Corinthians 8:1). It leads us away from love and into pride. It also allows us to maintain a distance from God while appearing religious. God freed us of our sin in order that we may see fully His desires for us and give ourselves completely to Him.

When you read the Bible, ask God what it is that He wants to share with you that day. Interact with the passage. Imagine what was going on and what the people were thinking. Receive the promises as if they were spoken for you. Ask God if you really believe them as true. What is holding you from complete and wholehearted trust in what He is communicating? Have the Bible reveal the secrets of your heart and attack the lies to transform your mind.

Communicating with God Not Just to God

Almost every Christian feels their prayer life is lacking. Again, it is viewed as a method instead of a relationship. We were taught how to pray using the ACTS method, which takes you through Adoration, Confession, Thanksgiving, and Supplication. This tool becomes a framework for how people pray. Unfortunately most Christians never graduate past it, but instead add to it. Their prayer list increases with all of the good things needing prayer. The lists include family, friends, their church, missionaries, people who are sick, people who are in need, the government, local government, their kid's school system, and on and on.

As the prayer list increases, the whole act of prayer becomes just something that needs to be checked off. A, C, and T of ACTS are moved through quickly to get to the items that need "the real attention". The thought of sitting still and listening becomes an additional burden of something to add to the list. No longer can you just knock it out; you have to sit still and wait. How long do we have to wait? What if God doesn't speak?

What is the purpose of prayer? Is reading through a list really prayer anyhow? Just as in reading the Bible, the focus is on spending time with God. Paul tells us to pray without ceasing (1

Thessalonians 5:17). He wasn't encouraging us to constantly read over our prayer lists. In everything ask God what He wants to do in that moment. When you want to spend specific time in prayer, ask God what He wants you to talk to Him about. If you feel burdened for a specific issue, tell Him about it. Ask Him what you should pray regarding it.

Prayer is not you trying to win back God's favor; it is you participating in the favor He has for you. Delight in God. Have God delight in you. Ask Him what He wants you to know. Once you realize how much God loves you, you will never neglect spending time with Him because it will become your life and fuel for life. Prayer removes you from the burdens of life and resets your priorities on the eternal and real.

Worshipping to Realign Your Heart

Worship also has the same effect of redirecting your focus off of yourself and circumstances and unto Jesus. With this renewed focus, worshippers get well. Worship increases your trust in Jesus that He has your best interests at heart. Therefore you are more willing to trust Him. If you don't fall in love with Jesus than you will not be willing to go through the steps He takes you through to get well.

Worship also changes you. It takes the truths of God and allows them to seep down into your heart. Each time you sing out the words of love to God and from God, you are making agreements to them. I remember, during one worship session where we were singing "Days of Elijah," there is one point in the song where we repeat the phrase, "There's no God like Jehovah." We got to the twelfth time repeating this phrase, and my heart just connected with God's. My eyes started to tear up and my heart started to race. What just happened? Holy Spirit rose up in me and connected to my current awareness. Within that moment I experienced a shift deepening my relationship with God. And, all I was doing was singing a seemingly simple truth. If you want healing from addiction, I don't believe you can neglect this step.

Believing God Can Do Immeasurably More Than We Ask or Think

One of the most devastating comments many with addictions face is being told you just need more faith in Jesus in order to be healed. As if the addiction is not shameful enough, calling out the person's faith is demoralizing. If all I need is faith as big as a mustard seed to move a mountain, imagine how small my faith is that I can't stop sinning.

Faith is our constant gaze on our Savior. You can have a huge faith, but if you get distracted and break your connection with Jesus, it is easy to fall. Life is full with many dangers, and we are learning to keep our gaze on the lover of our soul. Don't beat yourself up over mistakes or loss of focus; just keep at it. If you don't allow yourself to be discouraged, over time you will just continue to get better and better.

Thinking Your Way to a Better Lifestyle

"Finally, brothers and sisters, whatever is true, whatever is noble, whatever is right, whatever is pure, whatever is lovely, whatever is admirable—if anything is excellent or praiseworthy—think about such things." – Philippians 4:8

Often people believe that it is okay to let the mind wander. "I'm not really going to act on this, but I will enjoy thinking on it." These fantasies can be just as dangerous as the lies we believe.

These fantasies actually identify the lie: that sin is more enjoyable than following God.

Take every thought captive. The things you let your mind dwell on are the things you train your heart to want. God wants to fill our minds with His truth and reality (Galatians 6:7-8). You will never overcome addiction if you maintain fantasies of going back.

This is not to say that you beat yourself up every time your thoughts or dreams go there, but come back to God each time. Treat it as sin. Here is a sample prayer:

> *"Lord, I confess I entertained thoughts that were not Yours. I choose to think about good things instead. I want everything You have for me. Thank You for the forgiveness I have received."*

Saying No to the Sinful Act

Don't misunderstand everything that has been said thus far; there is still something to just not doing the behavior. Part of reprogramming yourself is to stop doing the behavior. You have had a lifetime training yourself in the addiction, therefore, you will need time to reprogram your thinking. Even if you get the triggers all healed up, you will still have an inclination to fall because that is what you have trained yourself to do. Also, the mere act of abstaining from sin will open you up to feel what is actually going on in your heart. The point is not to just change the behavior, but by changing the behavior, you can more clearly hear what God is trying to say to you.

It will be hard at first. It may feel very painful. You are learning something new. Don't be discouraged. You have been given everything you need for life and godliness (2 Peter 1:3). Take a stand. Use it.

Partnering with God to Impact Others

Sometimes it is good to start helping others. With everything there is a balance, but with service you get your eyes off yourself. You get your focus off your problems and start seeing yourself as a valuable asset to society. Addictions have a tendency to lead people into depression, and depression is strengthened and maintained by living in isolation. Service gets you out of your shell and allows you to interact with those around you. You also get to see that you bring something to the table that's a help, which can get you to start believing what God says about you – that you are significant and created with purpose.

Also stepping into other people's lives places you in the heart of God. We are to love God and to love others. Service puts you in partnership with God and positions you for an encounter with Him. These encounters are just as healing for you as offering life to the people to whom the service is directed. Addiction may have removed you from some levels of leadership while you are still in the midst of the battle, but it should not remove you completely from all levels of ministry. You still have something to offer others, and God has something for you in it.

Being Known By Others

Helping others is the first step out of isolation. But since it can be done without any true communication, accountability is a greater step. The humiliation and guilt of addiction erodes our self-esteem and breeds deviousness and manipulation as a means of not letting our real selves to be known. Shame of sin can only be healed once it is exposed and met with acceptance.

Doesn't God already know us completely? Why then do we hide? We are afraid that He might expose it and shame us some more. We are afraid He may confirm our fears of rejection and unloveliness. God is not hiding from us; He wants to be known. He wants to heal us so we can experience the abundant life He is offering.

Self-exposure to a group of committed friends attacks the fear of rejection head on. A response of acceptance and love can be more healing than just about anything else. To share the things which we feel should bring us rejection and instead have it foster greater intimacy is powerful.

Accountability should not be about how well you maintained purity. It is about reminding you of who you are in Christ. One of the best things you can do in accountability groups is to set aside time when you are together to speak God's truth over one another. As a group member, it endears you to the others as you remind yourself of how God sees that person, but it also sows life into the group that can easy be deflated by the act of exposure. This is so important to your healing that the next chapter is devoted to its significance.

Tools in Your Toolbox

It is very easy to focus on a list of things and think you need to do this or that to get better. Just remember a fairly simple equation, the more you get to know Jesus; the better you are. It is really that simple. You may still make mistakes. You may still hurt people. But as you focus in on Jesus and what He says about you, all the behavior will eventually fall in line.

The topics of this chapter are tools to help you focus more on Jesus rather than your pain or addiction. If your focus is merely getting better, your behavior may change quicker, but you will be trading one addiction for another. Not dealing with the root issue can only delay your ultimate healing. Jesus wants you healed, whole, and free. Jesus started His ministry stating this very thing.

> *"The Spirit of the Lord is upon me, because he hath anointed me to preach the gospel to the poor; he hath sent me to heal the brokenhearted, to preach deliverance to the captives, and recovering of sight to the blind, to set at liberty them that are bruised, To preach the acceptable year of the Lord." — Luke 4: 18-19*

Jesus came to heal the brokenhearted, deliver captives, restore sight, and bring freedom. He is not looking to merely correct behaviors. He is restoring you to who you were created to be. If this is Jesus' goal, He will bring it about to completion (Philippians 1:6). Jesus gave a specific tool to bring about this completion when Lazarus rose from the dead. We will look at this next.

10

RELATIONSHIPS CAN HEAL YOU

Jesus Provides the Healing; the Body Applies It

The goal of this book is to get you completely free from addiction. The tools mentioned already have created a path toward your healing, but you will never make it to the destination without relationships. Jesus is willing to raise you from the dead, but He wants others to help you remove the burial clothes (John 11:43-44).

This will be the hardest part to put into practice for some. Addiction is tied directly to shame, which motivates us away from others. We have become so good at keeping a distance that we only venture out of our self-made walls to take what we need from others. Addiction is by its very nature an attempt to get our needs met on our own. "I will take this from over here. I will take this from you. I will grab whatever it takes to quickly satisfy this ache I feel."

This is why so many of us want to deal with our addictions by ourselves. We are afraid to let others in on what we are thinking and feeling. We justify it by saying, "it's just God and me." We think this is a Christian attitude because the cross is sufficient for me. This is not how God intended. It is through relationships that we work out our salvation. Nearly 60 times in the New Testament we have commands that are tied to "one another." The majority of them are to love one another. We can't say we love God and hate our brother (1 John 4:20). It is through relationships with others that we see how well our relationship with God has taken root in our lives.

For most of us, it was through painful relationships that we formed the lies and behaviors that led us to addiction. However it is through healthy relationships that we are able to break off the addictions. This part is very important. Healthy relationships are going to give us the freedom for which we are looking. There is an interesting part of the story of Jesus raising Lazarus. Jesus calls him out of the grave, but it is the Jews that were comforting Mary that were told to remove Lazarus' grave clothes (John 11:44). What an amazing imagery for us. Jesus has removed sin from us, but we need to get the reminders of sin and those things pulling us back into sin removed by those who care for us. Complete healing is found and maintained by the relationships we have with others.

Last Step of My Healing

I believe that this is the one thing that has been the biggest hindrance to my complete healing. After experiencing a huge jump in my healing and bringing things out in the light, I never sought out close relationships to continue the process. I had dealt with many root causes but I still felt the need to maintain purity or lose my marriage. I could go 9 to 12 months without looking at pornography before losing focus. Knowing that hiding things was the path to further bondage, thankfully it would be brought in the open, but then I would go into two weeks of guilt and shame. I was doing so much better; but it was still painful.

I needed close friends with whom I could open up and share. I needed men who knew me and also had a heart of love that could receive slips as redeemed and not men who heard my faults as needing to be corrected and purified. I needed men who were not afraid to go deep into my heart and would love me no matter what they found there. I needed people that would show me that I wasn't too messed up. I needed people to make me feel normal. I needed people that would help me see the love of Jesus for me.

These people are hard to find. They were particularly hard for me as we kept moving around. Nine times within the first ten years of marriage we moved. This made it difficult to develop and maintain relationships outside of our marriage. Thankfully my wife and I were close friends, but those same-sex relationships, which are so valuable for complete healing, were missing.

David and Jonathan

The Old Testament tells a wonderful story of friendship through the man after God's heart and his soul mate, Jonathan. If you remember David raised his hand volunteering to fight the Philistine, Goliath. God worked a miracle, and David takes him out with a sling and a stone. David cuts off Goliath's head than chases the rest of the Philistine army with the head in his hand.

Saul turns to his commander and asked who David was. Nobody knew, so when David comes back, the commander brings him to Saul. David tells his story to Saul in the presence of Saul's son, Jonathon. Having heard David speak, Jonathan became one in spirit with him (1 Samuel 18:1).

Jonathan also loved the Lord and had tasted of what it was like to have God come on him in power. Jonathan had taken his armor bearer up into the Philistine camp, two against an entire army, and he trusted God's provision of handing their enemies over to them. So, when he heard David's faith, Jonathan knew he found someone he wanted to be near. In an instant the Bible says Jonathan loved David as himself. And we know that David also loved Jonathan.

These two men found a kindred spirit between them. They loved God and believed He would act on their behalf. And, they knew that they became more alive together. Those things God sparked in their hearts were fanned into flame in the other's presence. Friends are made to do that for you. They are to awaken God's Spirit within you and call out the desires God placed there.

Finding a Friend Takes Being Intentional

So where do you find this type of friend? You have to start by intentionally looking. Look for someone you admire, someone who is vulnerable, and someone who has time. More than likely it will not just happen. You will need to be intentional. Make time for others. Talk. Listen.

Friendship was an easy thing back when I was single. I had plenty of free time. I could hang out with different people every night and find people with whom I liked to do things. College was the place I formed a majority of my relationships and friendships. Now that I am married with kids, free time is a luxury that's hard to find. But, relationships are still very important; I have to make them work in order to maintain my freedom.

I may wake up earlier than I want. I may try a few activities I don't enjoy. Whatever it costs, I try out people that could be friends. For each person, keep inviting them to go deeper with you until either you realize you don't connect, you hit a level they want to stop, or you find a lifelong friend. If you hit a stopping point in the friendship level, honor where they are and enjoy what they can provide. It's not a personal attack against you; just keep looking for those people with whom you can go deep.

Friends Come in a Variety of Sizes

There was a guy I wanted to "try out." We had done some family activities together, and I wanted to see if he was someone with whom I could be a closer friend. I arranged to go running with him on certain mornings. Now, even though I am athletic, I have never enjoyed running. Nevertheless I viewed this as an opportunity to get to know him better. It gave us shared experiences and some inside jokes, and we became better friends.

While it was fun, I also learned that he was not willing to go to the depth I wanted. And although I was still left looking for a close friend that I could share my dreams and desires, I had still met someone I could enjoy being with. We need several people to meet several needs. Be willing to let someone meet a need for which they are suited without making them meet your every need. It will allow you to enjoy the people God gives you in life without resenting them for what they are not able to provide. If there is a hole in your relationships, then continue to pray to God for that need. He wants to satisfy your needs more than you do and He has promised to do so.

Help is Found in Others Who Have Traveled Your Road

Addictions are more obvious in the Christians landscape than ever before. No longer can you think you are the only one who understands your struggles because the church is filled with those who struggle. The great benefit of these people is they will not condemn you. They know their own struggles and battles with sobriety so they are quick to offer friendship in the midst of yours. Connect with them.

This type of group provides you a place to share your thoughts, struggles, fears, and dreams while not being judged. This is so important. If you don't have people to process what going on inside of your head, these thoughts will remain a tangled web mysteriously motivating your actions. This group will help you untangle that mess and help you pinpoint areas that are motivating destructive behavior. Remember the outward sin is not the main concern; it is the underlying motive of the heart that is driving the sin. When that motive is brought to the light and can be exposed to the love of Christ, true healing can take place.

Also when you allow others to know the deep things going on in your head, you will start to realize that you are not hopelessly evil as you may have feared. These fears force people into isolation through addiction. Addiction in a way soothes the pain of isolation by either dulling the senses or giving a false relief to the pain. People struggling with addiction need to be reconnected to God, others, and self. Radical honesty with others that will love, honor, and not condemn will pave the road to recovery.

A Right View of Sin

Whatever group of friends you gather, you don't want it to be a time of condoning sin. Sure, you also don't need your friends to be condemning you, but sin still hurts everyone in your life. There is no such thing as a private sin, no matter how much it may feel like it. Satan only needs a small foothold in order to keep you from your full destiny.

Ideally you want to find one person for the group who has conquered addiction in their own life to offer hope for the group's process. Someone who has battled their way to healing will have a healthy hatred for the destructive power of addiction. Sin is not something that they would want to play around. They will have confidence in the battles they have won and stand firm against going back.

I have also found that those who have had quick recoveries are not empathetic to those who struggle with their own healing. They also tend to have had a one-trick approach to the recovery process. This is not to say you should avoid them, they have something you may need. But you also need to protect your heart from anyone who wields the sword of shame.

For more resources of what to look for or to join one of my online men's groups, check out Prayer-Coach.com/bf.

An Easy Way to Grow Friendships

God loves each and every person. If we are to be like the One we love, then we also will love them. The great thing is He will help us with this. We can ask God what He loves about others. God loves sharing secrets about His children to those who will listen. These secrets are not people's hidden fears or private sins; God likes to share those things He likes about others. He wants us to know these secrets so that we would love them too.

Whatever group you are part of, you need to make sure that a regular part of your time with those people is to ask God what He likes about each person. The last few years I have been a part of groups that have done this, and I had never been a part of groups that loved each other so deeply. We were constantly being made aware of who each man was created to be. These reminders helped us see beyond the life we were currently living and pray into who God planned us to be – who we really are when we live out of our true self.

Here are some benefits to talking to God about the greatness of people in your group:

- God likes to show off the greatness of those He loves.
- We stop focusing so much on those things that we don't like about others. Instead, we look at what's good about them.

- We have believed the lies about how bad we are, and God wants other people to confirm those things that are good in us.
- God knows as we see the good in others, we will start to love them as He loves them.

People love others that believe in them. These relationships will call you out of addiction and into the life God created you to live. Once you have revealed everything in yourself that you assume would drive people away and only find acceptance and love, you will start believing in the great promises in the Bible about you. We are called to give life to others. Condemnation will lead people away from God and keep them from finding freedom. Hope and life will make people want to live to the fullness of who they are. He who has the most hope has the most influence. He who has the greatest faith in you will have the greatest impact on your life.

Blueprint For Accountability Groups That Works

God created us and placed within each of us a unique way to express God to this world. We are each amazing because God made us (Psalm 139:14). However most of us never live out of who God made us to be. We are either embarrassed by weaknesses or fearful that people will think we are prideful for expressing our strengths. Therefore we live in this lukewarm middle barely expressing the full nature of what God put in us.

If you want an accountability group to work, your focus is to live completely out of how God made you and not obsessed with corralling sin. Your goal is to be radically known. You need to remove all fear of someone finding out something about you. Fear will keep you from being free.

One model in which you can look at your life is the Johari Window, developed by Joe Luft and Harry Ingham. They determined that in your life there are things you know and don't know about yourself. And, in your relationships there are things that you reveal and things you hide from others. These distinguishing marks created four quadrants that I believe will help you radically gauge your accountability groups.

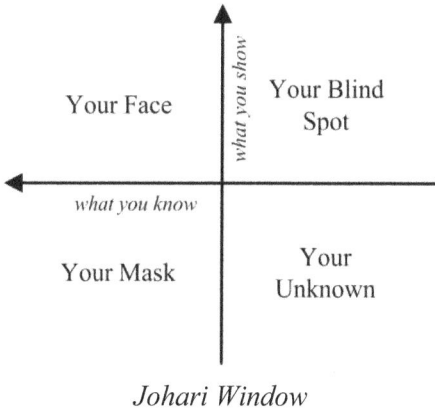

	what you show	
Your Face		Your Blind Spot
← *what you know*		
Your Mask		Your Unknown

Johari Window

Area 1. Your Face

This is what you know about yourself and what you reveal to others. This is what you like about yourself and believe others would also appreciate. This is the place you live out of.

Area 2. Your Mask

This is what you know about yourself but decide to hide from others. These are those things you are embarrassed about or fearful will cause rejection from others. Typically it is our sin that we hide, and although sin is not our true self, hiding the sin also hides the reasons the sin sprouted in our life.

Area 3. Your Blind Spot

This is what you don't know about yourself, but others are picking up on. These can be positive or negative. It could be that your even-keeled demeanor may come off as lazy to others around you. Or, you may have a real gift of teaching that you never knew.

Area 4. Your Unknown

This is area that nobody really knows about you yet. This untapped region may unlock keys you need to take you into God's destiny for you. The more you are scared of being known, the more is going to be hidden here.

The goal of accountability group is to make area 1 as big as possible. The more you live out of who God made you to be, the more He is going to resource you to do what He has created you to do. The Holy Spirit is drawn to people living out of who God made them to be. The way to make this area larger is to reveal those things you tend to hide and allow others the right to share the things they see in you. As you do this, more of your unknown becomes known.

Stopping sin is too small a goal for any group. Plus if you happen to attain that goal, what's the point of maintaining the relationships? People need to know others care about them. If you're only interested in your own healing, it will not make others feel they can be vulnerable or open.

With the goal of enlarging the area that you know about yourself and are willing to share, here are some ways to put them into practice during your group time:

1. Limit the group between 4-8 members. If you have more than this, encourage the start of a new group. More than 8 people allow people to hide and get away with not sharing.

2. Commit to come each week. Each week builds off the other. If people are in and out, it limits the openness of the group. Obviously people do get sick and sometimes have to travel, but this should be the exception.

3. As the leader start each group with some short motivation for the benefits of opening up. Remind people of the purpose. This is a new way of interacting with others—keep the vision in front of them.

4. Have each person share for 5-6 minutes. Time them. Some will need the timer to limit their comments; others will need it to encourage them to share more. The goal of the sharing is not to tell about their day, but to reveal things other people would not know about them. These should be struggles, dreams, hopes, dilemmas, directions, etc.

5. As the leader you should strive to be the most vulnerable in the group. You cannot expect the others to go where you don't lead them. You don't have to have all the answers; you are just showing the pathway. That pathway is vulnerability and love.

6. After someone shares others may ask clarifying questions to help them understand. This is not a time of correcting or fixing others. Trust God to bring their healing. The main thing they need is to feel accepted when sharing vulnerable areas of their life.

7. Pray God's heart over people. This is still not a time to correct others. Take each person before the throne of God and listen to what He has to say. Your words should be encouraging, comforting, and strengthening. If they are not, you are not hearing God's words for them. You may need to limit the length of prayers due to time. Listen to see if God is highlighting a particular person who may need more encouragement.

8. The prayer time is extremely important. It is not only for the person receiving prayer. While that is encouraging to them, the prayers allow the rest of the group to hear God's heart for them. It increases the affection for each person and seeing each of them as the amazing friend of God they were created to be. This allows you to have hope for one another and to see your need for that person.

9. Time outside of group will enhance the quality of sharing during the group. Spending time together outside group builds trust and shows appreciation for the person and not just the group.

These group times take two hours each week. When done right people look forward to group time and not ready to leave when it is over. A group like what I mentioned here creates space for you to process the other suggestions in this book.

If a group like this interests you but don't know how to find one, feel free check out Prayer-Coach/bf. I believe for some of you, this is the point that will push you into the freedom you want. I would like to help any way I can.

Some of you reading this book are reading it particularly to help a spouse or friend with an addiction. You also feel the desire to help any way you can. The next chapter leads through some points for you. Take courage there are ways you can help.

11

WHAT SHOULD I DO AS A SPOUSE OR FRIEND?

God's Purpose for Marriage

If relationships are what heal us, then your spouse has the power to bring the greatest healing in your life. This chapter will look at the view from the spouse or friend who wants to walk someone through their healing process. You are extremely powerful and can help make the process faster or slower.

In the garden God said it was not good for man to be alone. Man had perfect communion with God, but God said He was alone. Then He creates woman as a help-mate for him. The answer to man's loneliness was not more of God; it was woman. Isn't that strange?

Unfortunately, it did not take long before the oneness between man and woman was jeopardized. The forbidden fruit was eaten; shame and blame entered the garden. Separation occurred between God and man, but it also occurred between man and women. "This woman, she…"

When we got married, almost all of us thought our spouse would be the answer to the pain in our lives. They were the miracle drug to end all of our loneliness. Unfortunately, while it can be our greatest pathway to our freedom, marriage is more often the source of greater loneliness.

God created marriage for oneness, but sin distorts God's plan. Sin and shame keep us from moving out of the shell we have created to protect us from exposure and pain. As we remain isolated from our spouse, additional pain and shame are added to it. Then we pull away even more into our protective shell. We are on a deadly spiral, and we need something or someone to stop the bleeding.

God in His masterful plan usually puts two people together that are perfectly matched to heal all of the pain. The thing is that in order to enter into that healing there needs to be tiny deaths to self along the way. Are you going to choose to deny yourself to allow healing to flow to your spouse? When your spouse shares their struggles with impure thoughts, are you going to offer grace or shame? When your spouse tells you about their eating disorder, do you offer love or condemnation? When your spouse confides with you about their fears, do you offer words of life or dismiss them as unrealistic?

The right choices above are usually not easy because it is those areas of hurt in your spouse that feed the areas of hurt in your life. You have to choose life for your spouse because, even though attacking them feels like protecting you, it will hinder any chance of either of you finding freedom. Take your fears to Jesus. Allow Him to protect you. Then offer life to your spouse.

Jesus is better at protecting you than you are anyhow. It is through Him you are able to move toward oneness.

Perspective for the Journey

Many people with marriage issues face an emotional rollercoaster: good days and bad days. The good days are encouraging, but they are also emotionally draining because you just don't just know when the bad will come. Some days your spouse thinks you are the source of everything wrong; other days they are offering hope to something better.

What is going on? Is your spouse bi-polar? How come you don't know what you are going to get?

On those good days, your spouse is living out of their true self. All of God's works are wonderful therefore when our lives reflect the fruit of the Spirit, we are living out of who God created us to be (Psalm 139:14 and Galatians 5:22). Even if your spouse is not a Christian, deep down God has created in them the desire to have a good and healthy marriage with you.

Since this is God's will for your spouse, the enemy will try to steal, kill, and destroy it (John 10:10). He is feeding lies into your spouse about you, them, and your marriage. Therefore the ups and downs in your marriage are your spouse's choices over which voice they will listen to.

Now before you think this is only a matter of spiritual warfare, your spouse does have responsibility in the matter. And, choices they have made in the past allow the enemy greater influence.

Let's say your spouse had a father that constantly berated them by saying they would never amount to anything. Therefore they grew up with many lies about God and themselves. One lie might say God would never come through for them. What happens when there are difficulties in the marriage? The enemy feeds into those lies saying it is not going to work out. God is not going to protect you. You might as well give up. Your spouse is out to get you. They don't believe you will amount to anything anyway. You don't need that kind of pressure.

Because of the events of the past and the lies they already believe, the enemy's lies are now amplified to a degree that they cannot hear the voice of God.

What are you to do? Choose not to respond in like form. When they speak these lies to you, don't get angry. Don't defend yourself. Respond in love. Always proclaim your commitment toward the marriage. In prayer take authority over the enemy reducing his ability to speak to your spouse and to you. As you deny the

117

enemy's ability to speak, then the voice of God will be able to penetrate easier to your spouse. But also don't only focus on the negative; speak out life toward your spouse and the situation. Pronounce the words of God over them and invite more of the presence of God there.

This is not a magic pill. Your spouse still has the choice of whose voice to listen to. But you will be preparing the ground for a better harvest. You can plant the seed, till the ground, and water the plant, but only God can cause it to grow. It is the pleasure of God to change lives. And, even if your spouse decides not to change, God blesses those who choose to give life to others. Rest in His ability to protect and provide for you.

Unusual Hope of Divorce

Sometimes the best thing is for the marriage to end. Before you scream heresy telling me God hates divorce, please remember that while He does hate divorce, he still made concessions for it. When is divorce a good option? When the marriage is causing greater damage than a divorce.

This is not to be undertaken lightly, but far too many people are staying in a destructive marriage for fear of the wrath of God upon divorce. Let's not forget that God loves you. Jesus loves you enough to bear the cross for all the punishment of sin. He is not looking to see you in another form of bondage.

Let's face it; some people don't want to change. Some people want to stay in their sin, and their sin may cause pain in their spouse. A spouse who is willing to go outside marriage for their intimacy could bring repercussions into the family. A spouse who continues to wield abuse (physical, verbal, emotional, etc.) pulls the other further away from our loving Father.

Let me say this point again: consider heavily before venturing into divorce. I believe many things must be tried first. Confront your spouse about the pain they are causing. Try to seek professional help. Maintain a desire to seek reconciliation. Bitterness, anger, and resentment are not from the Lord, but love is not running back into danger. Love may look like anger to the other person, because you are no longer responding the way they want you to respond. Love may be a separation. Love may even be a divorce. "If you want to maintain that lifestyle, I will leave so you may continue on your way."

Although I do not desire to talk anyone into getting a divorce, I also don't want people to view themselves as a pawn that is expendable to the Lord. God treats His children with honor and love. He values them. Think about Joseph. He becomes a slave and a prisoner, but he never portrays himself as anyone other than royalty. His view of himself may have angered his brothers, but it also led to trust and respect from those who had been given earthly authority over him. He did not let himself be treated as merely a slave. When approached by Potiphar's wife, he denied her at his own expense. If we hold to a poor view of ourselves, than we will be treated poorly. If we hold to a Godly view of ourselves, it will force others to start treating us as honorable.

Example of Hope Emerging

I was able to get a close-up view of what this could look like one summer. My wife and I had a young lady, Anna, and her daughter stay with us because of troubles with her husband. She had been stuck in a belief that a wife was a servant of the husband. Her husband had the same mindset. They married a week after they met and she got pregnant on their honeymoon. As their daughter grew, the mother heart of protection for her daughter raised up. The pain that she had absorbed became too much to bear as it began to risk their child.

This is not an attempt to point any fingers. Both of them had destructive behaviors and a difficult background, but when she decided to change, he was not ready. Therefore when she left the house, he blamed her for everything. My wife and I could see her struggle with what she would believe. Was she doing the right thing? Should she just run back? Should she make him pay?

When you are dealing with the heart, it is never an easy road. Anna many times tried to work it out, but she also was doing it under a new mindset of who she was. She decided that if he started yelling at her, she would remind him not to speak to her that way, and if he continued she would end the conversation. Over time he realized she was not letting him talk to her that way anymore, which lead to more productive conversations.

This was not an easy road. Anna was a stay-at-home mom when she left. She had to find a job that provided childcare. She had to apply for financial help from the state. She had to find a home. She also had to find a lawyer to speak on her behalf. God's provisions were amazing, but He did not bring them back together. Life appears difficult for them, but God has brought His comfort and made a way.

The other amazing act of God is that Anna is able to work with her husband about sharing time with their daughter. They have learned how to make compromises for the other. Life may be hard, but it is currently better than she could have foreseen a year earlier. She can now believe God's heart for her and feel that He has a good plan even for her life.

Shame is Always Destructive

Once Anna had a different perspective on herself, the shame from her husband had less of an impact. Shame is a popular tool in our world because it often gives us immediate results. Even so, shame is a not tool in God's kingdom. You need to fight the tendency to shame your partner or friend into getting better. They are already getting enough of that from the enemy. Shame brings about hopelessness, which will not lead you to get better. Godly sorrow always comes from God and brings about repentance and no regret. When we try to force conviction on someone it brings about death and a desire for them to stay in regret. You will never get the spouse or friend God has for you if you keep them in regret and shame.

I understand the pain their sin caused you. All sin causes pain. Take that pain quickly to Jesus for Him to lift the burdens and be quick to forgive. As you do, you can be the source of life and healing.

If your spouse does not show any concern for your pain, they may not be a safe person to give yourself to at that time. Use wisdom and godly council. While your goal is reconciliation, your spouse's goal may not be, so thread carefully and be sensitive to the Spirit's leading.

Assuming your spouse is working on getting better, it is okay for them to see the pain it caused you, but don't make them carry it. Point them to Jesus and show them the way as you get the healing you need. This is a process. You more than likely will not be perfect throughout. Have grace on yourself and on them.

Hope for Things to Come

It is extremely important for you to ask God for the future possibilities for your spouse and your relationship. He has a plan for your lives. Search it out. Listen to our Father's heavenly wisdom and insight. The world and your flesh are telling you how you should view your spouse and your future together, but God in His goodness has an exciting and good plan for you. And, He wants to let you in on it.

You may get some of it through discernment. What are those things that originally drew you to this person? The good you saw only grows and gets better as they move closer to God. Ask your spouse what their dreams are. Those dreams are glimpses to the desires God placed in there.

As God gives you vision into who He has made both of you to be, remind your spouse of it. Call out their destiny. As they see that the future God has for them is something they want, they will become internally motivated to work through the things holding them back. It will also give you the resolve to not give up when it is hard, because you also desire that future God has for the two of you.

While the Bible is full of examples of people God used in spite of their sin, your full destiny is in life without sin. But greater still, God can redeem it all. He loves you and has a plan to get you to where all your dreams are fulfilled. Don't lose hope. Your spouse and friend can be completely free from addiction.

Conclusion

Life can be different. When Jesus said that I have come that you may have life and life to the full, He wasn't giving you false hope (John 10:10). This full life is not only for the very special people in God's kingdom; it is available for you and your friends. God has a good plan for you. Anything less than complete freedom is not worthy of the cross. Jesus has given you Himself; that is the abundant life. As we abide in Him, we naturally bear heavenly fruit. Addictions expose parts of your life where you haven't yet fully embraced or applied the life of Jesus within you. There is more God has for you.

I believe that the material in this book can help you achieve complete freedom from addiction. If you have any questions or desire help in this process, please check out more resources or reach out at ShorterJourney.com/bf. May your relationship with God and others go deeper as you put these things into practice.

Blessings!

12

10 THINGS TO PRAY FOR ADDICTION RECOVERY

Addictions can be very debilitating for the person and their family. My goal for this book is to give hope that complete freedom is available. The greatest thing people afflicted with addiction need is hope—hope life can be different and life can be better. This prayer list is written for those in addiction to pray over themselves, but it can just as easily be tweaked so friends and family can support their loved ones in addiction through their prayers.

The prayers are written as statements. Speaking them over yourself brings you into agreement with how God sees you, which will lead to a transformation of the mind. Pray knowing that this is God's will and He will answer your prayers.

1. I am forgiven and protected by God. I choose to release all those that have hurt me and bless them that I may pursue life.

2. My mistakes don't define me, but are transformed by the grace of God. Therefore I release shame off of me and receive love from God and others.

3. People who know the real me will never reject me because God says I am too awesome to reject.

4. I have not missed God's best for me, so I eagerly look to God for His vision of my future.

5. As I reveal what's going on inside of me, I will know true friendships and I will like myself more. Hiding leads to bondage.

6. As I look to God, He will lead me into right choices and give me strength and protection as I hold to those decisions.

Every small decision will either strengthen or weaken my ability to stay in freedom; therefore I will also trust God with them.

7. God loves me for who I am, and His love touches everything I experience. I will look for His love to me throughout my day.

8. God will lead me to people who I can trust to believe in me. People who I can enjoy and they can enjoy me.

9. Nothing can separate me from God's love and His grace is always available for me to access.

10. I can hear God's voice because He wants to speak to me.

I encourage everyone reading this book to declare these statements over themselves in agreement with God for the next 30 days. The truth will set you free only if you hold to the teachings (John 8:31-32). Train your mind and heart to believe these truths. We act out of what we believe. Daily declaring these truths will transform your thinking, which will change how you act.

ABOUT THE AUTHOR

Kevin Shorter is a prayer coach, writer, and mentor who helps people experience real freedom through a deeper connection with God. He wrote *Breaking Free* for those who love God, want change, and yet feel stuck in patterns that seem hard to escape.

Kevin is the voice behind the Prayer-Coach.com, where he regularly writes about prayer, identity, freedom, and learning to hear God's voice. His writing is grounded in Scripture and shaped by years of walking with people through seasons of struggle and growth. Alongside the blog, he sends weekly encouragement emails that offer simple truth, prayer, and perspective for everyday life. These messages are meant to remind people that God is near, kind, and actively at work in their story.

Kevin has led men's groups since the 1990s, and he continues this work today through online men's groups. He believes freedom was never meant to be pursued alone. These groups are safe, grace-filled spaces where men can be honest, pray together, and grow in lasting change. Consider joining at ShorterJourney.com/men.

Kevin is married to his wife Allison, and together they have served as missionaries in Turkey and China. These years shaped their faith, deepened their trust in God, and strengthened their call to help others walk closely with God. Kevin and Allison have two daughters, Rachel and Elizabeth, and family remains a central part of his life and ministry.

If you enjoyed this book, please consider writing a review or sharing it with your friends. This would be greatly appreciated. Thanks.

OTHER BOOKS
BY THE AUTHOR

The Prayer Book for Common People
Vol. 1: Why We Talk to God
Vol. 2: How to Talk to God

Discover new ways to connect with God through Scripture-based practices that make prayer more personal, creative, and life-giving. From listening to God's voice to praying with imagination, faith, and community, you'll find fresh confidence and freedom in your daily conversations with Him.

3,500+ Prayer Quotes: Inspiration to Draw You Closer to God

The desire of this book is to gather nuggets of wisdom from people who have spent time with God and journaled their findings. These quotes are intended to inspire us to continue our journey of faith and fan the flame of passion to spend time with God.

Academy of Powerful Caregivers: The Motivation of a Caregiver

The Academy of Powerful Caregivers contains practical steps to maintain confidence in your ability to help others. Whether you are a teacher, nurse, parent, pastor, missionary, or any other kind of caregiver, you will learn to build lasting help by looking at Paul's life and finding transferrable action points for your life.

Abundant Living: Two Hidden Truths in the Parable of the Sower Can Release You Into Abundant Living

See how Jesus prepared his disciples through teachings and real-life examples. Whether you are being sent out like the disciples or never leaving the city where you were born, God has an amazing adventure for you to stretch your faith and reward you with a greater connection with Him.

4 Steps to Supernatural Breakthrough in Prayer

God wants us to be experienced and will remove every barrier if we would just let Him. Walk through how faith, holiness, thanksgiving, and community will release you into intimacy with God. Get excited for this adventure with Him. He has more waiting for you.

Prayer Journals:
For Women: Embracing His Love
Leaning Into His Beauty
For Men: Growing Spiritually Strong
Empowering Your Faith

These journals not only give you space to write out your prayers, but they also contain sections to pull out thins you want to find quickly later. Each page contains prayer quotes to inspire you to continue pursuing God.

www.ingramcontent.com/pod-product-compliance
Lightning Source LLC
LaVergne TN
LVHW041225080426
835508LV00011B/1084